Falling Short of The Glory

Salome W. Thompson

AuthorHouse™
1663 Liberty Drive
Bloomington, IN 47403
www.authorhouse.com
Phone: 1-800-839-8640

Published by AuthorHouse 03/28/2012

ISBN: 978-1-4567-2866-3 (sc)
ISBN: 978-1-4567-2867-0 (e)

Library of Congress Control Number: 2011900297

Acknowledgments

To my dear mother, Ruthie "Tot" Williams, who has always gone beyond the call of duty, who has always listened, and who is always willing to give a hand, not just to her children but also to all who call upon her.

Thanks to each of my faithful family members, and to some special friends who believed in me and loves me dearly.

I dedicate this book to my father in the ministry, Rev. A. C. Mixon, who passed away before the completion of this project.

Contents

Foreword

Fallen Short

Salome Thompson has challenged us in these pages to take a long hard look at our lives to determine if our character is being developed day by day reflecting the life of Jesus the Christ. It is paramount that each believer has the utmost desire to not just talk the talk but more importantly walk the walk so others will see Christ in them and come asking what must they do to be saved and live a life full of joy, peace, love, understanding and POWER.

The WORD is the only thing we have to guide us, mold us and make us into believers that will live in the Holy of Holiest and not the outer courts. Your daily routine must include quality time in the WORD…Paul admonished us to "Study" to show ourselves approved…workmen that needed not be ashamed." Our walk will be strengthened as we meditate on WORD and as we hide it in our hearts.

Live so that others will know that you LOVE Him because all of your actions are a daily testimony to His goodness and mercy in your life. Join the spiritual witness protection program today.

James L. Davis,

Servant Bishop

Introduction

The Holy Spirit of Jesus Christ gave this book to me for his people. At the beginning of this process I thought it was for a sermon, but as I continued to write I knew it was more than just a Sunday morning message. There is an anointing of God on this book to help believers evolve from stagnant Christians into a royal priesthood. This will help people at this present time and for generations to come move into the sanctuary of God. The process depends on each individual. The process of a disciple is a renewed spirit and mind for the glory of God moving the believers from glory to glory. I know this information now rests in the hands of a lover of Christ, who will experience growth in his or her life.

In this writing, when I speak of "falling short," I'm referring to falling short of all the promises that we have from God. I am speaking of man accepting being any less than a conqueror and lacking the desire to be made in the image of God, when this image is clearly described through His word. Fallen human beings accept hell as their final destination and do not strive for glory. The fallen believe that being defeated, broke, and depressed is an acceptable option. Without the knowledge of the process, we will believe the voice of the enemy. The author of Hebrews 12:15 reminds us that we may fail to unite ourselves to the grace of God. *Looking diligently lest any man fail of the grace of God; lest any root of bitterness springing up in you, and thereby many be defiled*;

Webster's definition of the word fail means to fall short of an end or purpose, to be unsuccessful, to waste away. These are just a few of its meaning. You can fall and never experience His grace and His glory. In the fallen state, a person adopts an attitude of bitterness and the flesh dominates. Although each of us may fall, the Bible makes it clear that there is something you can do to rise from that position.

We learn by failing if we are wise enough to know that we have failed.

The wise man will learn from the errors of others and from the men in the Bible. That is one of the reasons it was written—so we may learn from them. Falling short of His glory means not fulfilling your full potential of walking in holiness and becoming the temple of God.

We have been called to become the temple of God. The temple molds us into becoming the priests of God so that Christ may dwell in us.

As we find in 1Pet.2: 4-5: *To whom coming, as unto a living stone, disallowed of me, but chosen of God, and precious, ye also, as lively stones, are built up a spiritual house, an holy priesthood, to offer up spiritual sacrifices, acceptable to God by Jesus Christ.*

The following passages explain that to become a temple we have to work and grow into it so that God can dwell in us by his spirit.

He is the one who holds the whole building together and makes it grow into a sacred temple dedicated to the Lord. In union with him you too are being built together with all the others into a place where God lives through his Spirit (Eph.2: 21-22). Fallen short is the problem that we have created, but

God has given us a purpose, a plan, and a promise.

Falling Short

It is a fearful thing to fall into the hands of the living God (Heb.10:31).

Wouldn't it be a dreadful thing to fall short of the glory of God, when the promise has already been given to you in the word of God? What happens if you don't know how to obtain the glory or the promises that belong to you? The promises of God are true and can be obtained in the life of all who believe in Him. The promises of God have gone forth from His mouth and it will not change. God will not change His promises to you for they are sure and Amen. In the book of Hebrews we are given the guidelines to obtain the promises. *For ye have need of patience, that, after ye have done the will of God, ye might receive the promise* (Heb.11: 36).

Faith is the founding principle in the life of a believer, or Christian. Man was given a measure of faith, and that measure is enough to exercise faith and put away unbelief. There are three levels of faith ascribed by Jesus in the Bible. That I will discuss briefly: no faith, little faith, and great faith. Those with no faith believe only when they see the results. The disciples displayed no faith when they were on the stormy sea with Jesus on board. They became so concerned about the ship sinking that they awoke Him and asked if He cared if they perished. Those with little faith believe as an emotional response and not as if it is the founding principle. Peter was one of them who had little faith. He saw Jesus walking on water and wanted to go to Him. He started walking on water; he saw the wind, became afraid and started to sink. However, those with great faith stand on the word when emotion, circumstance, appearance, and even their own minds contradict the word. The Roman centurion was one of the people who had great faith. The only thing he needed from Jesus was for him to speak the word. He was assured that his servant would be well. Faith works for us to the degree that we are willing to *activate* it. Activation is the only way to achieve the third level of faith in pursuit of holiness, and this can only happen through the love of Jesus. *But faith which worketh by love* (Gal. 5:6b).

The seed of faith that lies within you is like a grain of mustard. You have to bury it within you and no man can boast of it. As long as your faith is something to boast about, then it serves others little use. After the burial of a seed, that is when it takes root and grows into a tree. It is not until it is a tree that others may come and rest on it. The faith that you possess is for you to "bear the infirmities of the weak" and restore those who are overtaken in fault. When others rest in your faith and see your faith at work, then they too can live by faith. Bury it in the area of your life in which you want to see growth and maturity. Plant your faith in the word of God so that you will be able to help someone else. Do not plant your faith any longer in the stock trade, or in any other forms of gambling. Your faith may not look like much, but plant it anyway. Put your faith in the word of God, not in your own wisdom and strength, not in who you know or the position you hold. You can't go on to pursue holiness without being a disciple and knowing the power of the word.

Faith is manifested in our lives when we believe the word of God with our hearts or minds. The heart is the inner self that thinks, feels and decides. The heart is that which is central to a person. One's heart often reveals their true character or personality. This intellectual activity corresponds to what is called the "mind" in English. The mind is the part of a person that thinks and reasons. Both of these definitions are from the New Illustrated Bible Dictionary. We can only confess with our mouth when the heart or mind believes. The issues of life flow from the heart, so the mouth will say what the heart believes. Perhaps it is hard for you to believe the word because of the way you understand the power of the word. Once you fall in love with a person it is easier to believe what he or she says. Even if you know your spouse or child is lying, you will still believe them in spite of this knowledge. In the case of the spiritual, once we fall in love with Jesus and His word then believing in Him is easy. Jesus and His word are inseparable. Jesus is the word and the word is Jesus, who became flesh for us. Therefore, when I speak the word, I actually *speak* Jesus and everything that He represents. The word is the resurrected power of Jesus, which has spirit and life. When you have faith in His word, you will say what the word says about you, and not what the world say. *We having the same spirit of faith, according as it is written, I believed, and therefore have I spoken; we also believe, and therefore speak.* (2Cor. 4:13) Therefore the promises of God are real. Love alone will ultimately allow us to wait, in the hope that the righteousness of Christ in faith will manifest itself in our lives. That's the faith that will make you strong and give you perfect soundness (i.e., nothing missing and nothing broken). *And his name through faith in his name hath made this man strong, whom ye see and know: yea, the faith which is by him hath given him this perfect soundness in the presence of you all* (Acts 3:16). Choose which level of faith you will activate in your life. God has given you an offer and the choice is yours. Who will you choose?

The greatest loser is one that doesn't believe the word of God. We fall short when we do not have faith in the word. There is only one thing to do to keep from falling short—be like David and Paul. These great men desired only one thing in their hearts and minds. Let's take a brief look at their desires.

David's desire was communion with God. He understood that in seeking God, he had to do it wholeheartedly. Sometime in life you can have a passion for something and don't know how to pursue it. There are also cases whereby you do not discern the spirit that is speaking to you. Then that same passion can be driven in the wrong direction, which only bring you harm, hurt, despair and distress. David realized the passion that was within him and did not turn that affection to the things of the world to fulfill that passion. He understood the need and made his pursuit of the Lord his top priority. He wanted to worship God in the house for the rest of his life, not just on days that he felt good. David knew that as he worshiped God, he would gain wisdom and knowledge. He would look to see the joy and pleasure that His beauty brought.

Paul's desire, on the other hand, was to fulfill his heavenly calling in Christ Jesus. Each believer must believe, as Paul did, that if they finish the race they would get a prize. As Paul did, we should focus all our attention on the pursuit of the one fundamental principle: building upon and allowing everything to be centered on Christ Jesus. Paul accomplished this by letting Christ direct their ongoing relationship by His skillful hand. Once a relationship begins with God, it has to be a continuous process, because the believers have not reached the level of obedience unto death, as Christ did. The falling short of the glory occurs because the believers failed to continue the process of becoming the image of God.

You don't have to be a loser! You can walk into the holy profession as an ambassador. Webster's defines "ambassador" as a special, accredited representative who is on a diplomatic mission. Each country sends an ambassador to foreign nations to represent their native country, for the purpose of making peace. A nation's leader would never knowingly send criminals or scoundrels to conduct the affairs of the nation; they send those who share their beliefs and values. It is the same in the spiritual world. Our purpose as representatives is to bring forth the message from the Most High God and show Him as Christ. We were sent by God to bring forth the message of love, joy, and peace to a dying, lost world. To do so we must live lives that represent the one who sent us. Then, when the world sees Christ in us, they too will want to become His representative. The author of Proverbs tells us, *A wicked messenger falleth into mischief: but a faithful ambassador is health* (Prov.13: 17).

We fall short when we allow the power of God to work in and through us and then think we have done something of our own power. Once we do that we have withheld the glory of God for ourselves. He has given unto us all the power we need to live a godly life and have dominion over our environment. The glory of God is His presence, His greatest and His authority. The glory of God also relates to power and honor. Let me explain. God's glory has been revealed to us through nature, and everything that we see was created out of nothing. The glory of it is God. The very characteristic of God is His glory. Jesus said if we believe we shall see this same glory. We as a body of believers always think that God is going to take something away from us when in fact He only wants to give you an abundant, eternal life. Eve was deceived because she thought that God was trying to keep something away from her, when in fact He had already given it to her. God has already given us glory, because Jesus prayed that He would in John 17:22. *And the glory which thou gavest me I have given them; that they may be one, even as we are one:* The glory of God comes to us when we are obedient to Him in whatever task He has assigned to us. We bring Him glory when we have finished the course and have done it with joy. Then, God gives us the glory and honor we have given to Him day by day. If we withhold the glory for ourselves, here on earth, then we will have our reward now.

One day a friend and I were visiting the patients at the local hospital. On this particular day, we were led by the spirit to go into each room and offer prayer to the sick. Our goal was to be a blessing to those who were sick and also to their family. To our surprise, there was an elderly, frail, white-headed gentleman in the bed. He welcomed us into his room and gladly accepted the prayer. At the end of the prayer he started worshipping God. In return this elderly man was a blessing to us. The one thing that this man said to God was, God, I don't want your glory. Years later and neither one of us have forgotten this statement. This taught us early in ministry not to want or take the glory that belong to God. I will give God all the glory and not hold any back for myself. In John 13:31-32, Jesus said, *Now is the Son of man glorified, and God is glorified in him. If God be glorified in him, God shall also glorify him in himself, and shall straightway glorify him.* Another way of saying this is, if I glorify the Father and the Father is glorified in me, then the Father will glorify me himself. The responsibility of receiving glory should not be a priority of ours but will be granted as we do what we are ordained to do. The heart of the believer is not to receive the glory, but his heart is to please his heavenly Father. For these reasons we should give God all the glory and honor that belong solely unto Him. (For additional reference, see John 17:1–5; 24.)

The power of Jesus manifests itself through people. The power comes through us, but it is from God. The power is not ours to do with as we please. Humble yourself, as a child to his parent, believing and trusting every word that was written. After we have humbled ourselves, we need to know how to apply the power of the word and to activate the Holy Spirit into our life in order to see Jesus manifested. We must learn how to operate effectively in the dominion in which we live. Without knowledge or understanding of this dominion, we will continue to repeat history, just like Eve.

In the Christian journey we will fall short! Not only does the Bible say it, but also I can provide examples of men who have fallen short since the race was started. However, during this continuous process we experience growth, which leads to the development of the characteristics that God wishes to see in each one of us. We develop not only so we can change into the glorious image of God but also so we have the wisdom and knowledge to be our brother's keeper. Being my brother's keeper happens not in word only but also in deeds.

In order to be my brother's keeper, I first have to abandon my own sensual desires. Without the change, I can't see the value in my brother, because I haven't been able to see the value within myself. In all the ways we change, and in all that we become, it is for the glory of God and for us to be as Christ in all things—that is, to accept and walk into a holy and reverent fear of the most-High God. Follow the Golden Rule: "Do unto others as you would have them do unto you."

Lord, Make Me a Sanctuary

The earliest sanctuary was known as the tabernacle, also called the temple, which served as a place of worship. The Lord said to Moses, *And let them make me a sanctuary that I may dwell among them* (Ex. 25:8). God gave specific instructions for the design and furnishing of the tabernacle that would house His presence. The tent, which was the first structure for worship for the Israelites, was a moveable building. God later allowed Solomon to build a permanent structure, called a "temple," which would replace the tabernacle.

> *And it came to pass in the four hundred and eightieth year after the children of Israel were come out of the land of Egypt, in the fourth year of Solomon's reign over Israel, in the month Zif, which is the second month, that he began to build the house of the LORD. And the house which king Solomon built for the LORD, the length thereof was threescore cubits, and the breadth thereof twenty cubits, and the height thereof thirty cubits. And the porch before the temple of the house, twenty cubits was the length thereof, according to the breadth of the house; and ten cubits was the breadth thereof before the house. And for the house he made windows of narrow lights. And against the wall of the house he built chambers round about, against the walls of the house round about, both of*

the temple and of the oracle: and he made chambers round about: The nethermost chamber was five cubits broad, and the middle was six cubits broad, and the third was seven cubits broad: for without in the wall of the house he made narrowed rests round about, that the beams should not be fastened in the walls of the house. And the house, when it was in building, was built of stone made ready before it was brought thither: so that there was neither hammer nor axe nor any tool of iron heard in the house, while it was in building. The door for the middle chamber was in the right side of the house: and they went up with winding stairs into the middle chamber, and out of the middle into the third. So he built the house, and finished it; and covered the house with beams and boards of cedar. And then he built chambers against all the house, five cubits high: and they rested on the house with timber of cedar. And the word of the LORD came to Solomon, saying, Concerning this house which thou art in building, if thou wilt walk in my statutes, and execute my judgments, and keep all my commandments to walk in them; then will I perform my word with thee, which I spake unto David thy father: And I will dwell among the children of Israel, and will not forsake my people Israel. So Solomon built the house, and finished it. (1Kings 6:1–14)

As you can see, God provided full details for the design of every area of the temple. Yet we still say to God, "Make me a sanctuary," as if the words of the Old Testament were somehow outdated. The sanctuary that we are constructing today is the character of our lives, which must reflect Jesus. Just as it is with the tabernacle, so it must be with our physical body. Our body is the tabernacle, or sanctuary of God, which is a moveable tent. The earth is not our home, yet we must still go to all nations and make disciples of all men. He does not want man to construct the sanctuary without direction. In the Old Testament, he gave commandments and laws to live by. In the New Testament, He sent the Holy Spirit to construct the inner man as we yield to His direction. Most of the details from the Bible and the beautification of the temple were given for the holy place and the holy of holies that resides inside. The beauty of man is not the outer shell but the "inner man," which shows Christ.

The inner man is renewed day by day as we follow Christ: *In whom the god of this world hath blinded the minds of them which believe not, lest the light of the glorious gospel of Christ, who is the image of God, should shine unto them* (2 Cor. 4:4). Paul let it be known to all believers that as we change into the image of our Lord, the glory of God will radiate upon our faces, as it did upon the face of Moses. We are commanded to leave the outer courts (outer man), which is the flesh, because it is decaying. As the Holy Spirit affects our "inner man," we are changed, because we are dying to the flesh. Although death constantly surrounds us, we are kept by the renewal of the inner man. We are supposed to be changed and are changed: *For we which live are alway delivered unto death for Jesus' sake, that the life also of Jesus might be made manifest in our mortal flesh. So then death worketh in us, but life in you* (2 Cor. 4:11—12). This can only be done as we die in our flesh and the Holy Spirit becomes alive in us. *Having therefore these promises, dearly beloved, let us cleanse ourselves from all filthiness of the flesh and spirit, perfecting holiness in the fear of God* (2 Cor. 7:1).

All the work that goes on within the temple of man is the building, renewing, casting down, and tearing down of the inner man so that he will become the image of Christ. We have the ability to learn, to gather the secret and the hidden treasures of God by the revelation of the Holy Spirit. We have the skills to cope with a changing environment and the will to make changes. *For we know that if our earthly house of this tabernacle were dissolved, we have a building of God, an house not made with hands, eternal in the heavens* (2 Cor. 5:1). Paul makes it clear to us that the tabernacle of our earthly house --- our physical body, which is temporary --- will one day be replaced with a more permanent tabernacle made not by our hands. Jesus Himself came through this physical tabernacle during His earthly life. However, as the Bible says: *But Christ being come an high priest of good things to come, by a greater and more perfect tabernacle, not made with hands, that is to say, not of this building* (Heb. 9:11). Christ, therefore, has come and is the greater and more perfect tabernacle, not made by hands.

The first covenant was the worldly, or physical, sanctuary only; it signifies the present, and a figure of the future. *Then verily the first covenant had also ordinances of divine service, and a worldly sanctuary* (Heb. 9:1). But Christ came to show us a greater tabernacle, not made with hands. The tabernacle that we are to become, as he did, was not a building. Peter knew the time was coming that he had to cast off his human body, the tabernacle: *Yea, I think it meet, as long as I am in this tabernacle, to stir you up by putting you in remembrance; Knowing that shortly I must put off this my tabernacle, even as our Lord Jesus Christ hath shewed me* (2 Pet. 1:13—14).

We must also realize that that the day is coming when each of us must become that sanctuary for Christ. When we ask God to make us a holy place, to set us apart for His worship, God will say, "Okay, when are you going to start?" Jesus will say, "I would love that. That's the reason I died --- so you can become the sanctuary and live like me." Just as Christ is the expressed image of His Father and the brightness of His glory, so we must strive in our hearts to become the image of Jesus Christ. *Who being the brightness of his glory, and the express image of his person, and upholding all things all things by the word of his power, when he had by himself purged our sin, sat down on the right hand of Majesty on high;* (Heb. 1:3).

Jesus' death is an example of how we must forsake all to become the sanctuary of God. Jesus said, "I must die, but in three days I will rebuild the temple." This does not mean death at the hands of a Roman soldier or on the Roman cross, but rather death of the flesh for the sins of the world. We will also be resurrected to eternal life if we become, and remain, a living sanctuary of God.

Becoming a sanctuary depends on how much you are willing to pay for it, but in the end you will flourish: *The house of the wicked shall be overthrown: but the tabernacle of the upright shall flourish* (*Pro.*14: 11). Pay, in this context, does not refer to money but rather the amount of your life you are willing to surrender to God. The Lord wants mastery over your entire being. The book of Hebrews tells us how the sanctuary was a foreshadow of human beings. The design of the tabernacle suggests that the old man is to be reformed. As we reach the New Testament we see the word ingrained within us, written upon our heart, and we become the sanctuary of God. The word "sanctuary" also means the most holy place or the holy of holies.

The Holy Ghost this signifying, that the way into the holiest of all was not yet made manifest, while as the first tabernacle was yet standing: Which was a figure for the time then present, in which were offered both gifts and sacrifices, that could not make him that did the service perfect, as pertaining to the conscience; Which stood only in meats and drinks, and divers washings, and carnal ordinances, imposed on them until the time of reformation. But Christ being come an high priest of good things to come, by a greater and more perfect tabernacle, not made with hands, that is to say, not of this building. (Heb. 9:8—11)

Now that you are ready to become a sanctuary, let's start at the gates of reformation.

A Shadow of the Tabernacle

Mosaic Law and the system of the tabernacle was a shadow, not the very image. The New Testament explains to us that it was a mere model of things to come.

> *Who serve unto the example and shadow of heavenly things, as Moses was admonished of God when he was about to make the tabernacle: for, See, saith he, that thou make all things according to the pattern shewed to thee in the mount. (Heb. 8:5)*

> *For the law having a shadow of good things to come, and not the very image of the things, can never with those sacrifices which they offered year by year continually make the comers thereunto perfect. (Heb. 10:1)*

> *It was therefore necessary that the patterns of things in the heavens should be purified with these; but the heavenly things themselves with better sacrifices than these. For Christ is not entered into the holy places made with hands, which are the figures of the true; but into heaven itself, now to appear in the presence of God for us. (Heb. 9:23—24)*

The tabernacle and the human body are designed for worshiping God. Let us exam the body as a shadow of the tabernacle in the Old Testament. Both of them are divided into three parts (which we will look at in greater depths in the other chapters). The main rooms of the tabernacle are the outer courts (gates), the holy place, and the holy of holies. The human body consists of three main parts --- the body, the soul, and the spirit. The body has the ability to smell, taste, hear, see, and feel. The soul of the human body is the will, the mind, and the emotion. The spirit of the human body is the conscience. Let's talk about the body, the fleshly part of the human being and the spirit.

The Flesh

This is the place where any and every thing goes, nothing is killed in the natural and the spiritual man remained stagnant. We, as Christians, bring the world's system into those courts and tend to behave just as they do. This is the group that parties all weekend while singing in the choir or holding an office in the church. The preacher preaches to satisfy itching ears and receives the offering. These people will lie just to see the expression on your face. They spread gossip as fast as the newspaper. To these people, marriage means nothing, and adultery is common. They hate all the people around them that represent what is good. Yet they think because they come to church God should be pleased with them. They compete for positions in the church as people compete in a ballgame. Denying part of the Trinity is natural for these people. All that matters to them is becoming rich and famous, and they block out the word out after hearing it. They have ears but can't hear and eyes but can't see. Their hearts are cold and stony, and they lack understanding of the word. In this court, the world's opinion about us is more important than the word of God.

Why is it so easy to live up to the world's standard yet so hard to believe and live by God's standard? The Bible claims *no flesh should glory in his presence* (1 Cor. 1:29).

The Soul of Man

> *Our soul waiteth for the Lord: he is our help and our shield. For our heart shall rejoice in him, because we have trusted in his holy name (Pss. 33:20 –21).*

After we have sacrificed our heart, soul, and mind on the altar in the outer court, then transformation can take place. That living sacrifice has made you a whole man and now you can start experiencing the glorious manifestation of the Lord. The glory was seen when God was pleased with the sacrifice made to Him according to His plan. We see that the glory of the Lord filled the house when Moses completed the construction of the sanctuary. Another time, the glory of God was revealed after Solomon completed the temple. I believe in my heart that the glory will be seen again when we as individuals construct our temple unto the Lord according to His plan. If God revealed His glory once, then He has to do it again. This is the place where man has to cast down every thought that exalts itself against the knowledge of God.

> *Casting down imaginations, and every high thing that exalteth itself against the knowledge of God, and bringing into captivity every thought to the obedience of Christ. (2 Cor.10: 5)*

As the Bible describes it, all the splendor of the temple was concentrated on the inside. *So Solomon overlaid the house with pure gold: and he made a partition by the chains of gold before the oracle; and he overlaid it with gold. And the whole house he overlaid with gold, until he had finished all the house: also the whole altar that was by the oracle he overlaid with gold. And the floor of the house he overlaid with gold, within and without. And he carved thereon cherubims and palm trees and open flowers: and covered them with gold fitted upon the carved work (1Kings 6:21-22, 30&35) and* for more information see 1Kings 6: 15-38. Yet the inside will manifest itself on the outside, and this is seen all the time in the lives of people. We often work on the outside of our temple, forgetting the inside, where true beauty resides. Forgetting or refusing to furnish our inside will cause us to fulfill our lust for flesh, or our lust for approval, which is the world way of doing thing and that is what he offers. Then you will become a stagnant Christians because the living water is not continuously filling you up and overflowing. When we operate from the Holy Place, it becomes a joy to honor and respect God in our practice of worship. Once we move into the most holy place and taste of his goodness it is impossible to turn back to follow the world system of doing thing. Your constant focus shall be on bringing Him honor and glory. Only the officiator priests were allowed to enter the holy place. When we choose to die to our flesh under the subjection of the Holy Spirit, that is when we act as officiate priest over our body.

The Spirit

When you enter behind the veil, your flesh and imagination have no place to dwell in the sight of God.

> *For thus saith the high and lofty One that inhabiteth eternity, whose name is Holy; I dwell in the high and holy place, with him also that is of a contrite and humble spirit, to revive the spirit of the humble, and to revive the heart of the contrite ones. (Isa. 57:15)*

We, who are contrite spirit, only do the will of the Father and allow His kingdom to become on earth as it is in heaven. This is where the Ark of the Covenant, or Mercy Seat, is housed. The word has been tested and proven to be true by the time you reached this area. The holy of holies is the place where the spirit doesn't waver on the promises of God but stands as a concrete pillar. This spirit within you is ready for only the Master to use. Then you will know that you have been chosen, appointed, and ordained by God. The word of God will be alive within you and you will depend on Him for all provisions. This body has now become the temple, and the world will see the manifested light of Christ that is within you. *Let your light so shine before men, that they may see your good works, and glorify your Father which is in heaven* (Matt. 5:16). The word will come alive in the heart of man. In His presence which is the holy of holies is where Christians are as transparent as Christ is. The image of God is transparent because every thing that God is can be seen in the Bible and all over the earth. The righteousness of God is reflected in our life when we treat man, as God wants them to be treated. We are transparent, so that others can see God through us and also so that man can see that we once were in a fallen state but the grace of God had redeemed us.

Peter encourage us to make the necessary changes while we are still in this tabernacle, as the older members of the church would say it, do it while the blood is still running warm in your veins.

Yea, I think it meet, as long as I am in this tabernacle, to stir you up by putting you in remembrance, Knowing that shortly I must put off this tabernacle, even as our Lord Jesus Christ hath shewed me (2 Pet.1: 13-14). This is one of the things the Holy Spirit wants us to implement and practice so that we may become a suitable temple for the Master's use. We were predestined to become the temple, to reflect His glory and have the character of God.

Becoming a living sacrifice, which is your reasonable service, helps us achieve a transparent temple.

Temple of God

Paul wrote to the Corinthians, "For ye are the temple of the living God." This has to be more than just words to you. You have to see these very words, as Jesus Himself and you can become that temple that serve God alone.

> *And what agreement hath the temple of God with idols? For ye are the temple of the living God; as God hath said, I will dwell in them, and walk in them; and I will be their God, and they shall be my people. (2 Cor. 6:16)*

The Revelation of Jesus Christ was given to John for us so that we may know that the tabernacle of God is with man. *And I heard a great voice out of heaven saying, Behold, the tabernacle of God is with men, and he will dwell with them, and they shall be his people, and God himself shall be with them, and be their God (Rev.21: 3).* Therefore if you fail to construct a temple now how are you going to dwell in His presence later because John also saw no temple? The temple is made up of the Trinity and all who has become one with Christ. *And I saw no temple therein: for the Lord God Almighty and the Lamb are the temple of it (Rev.21- 22).* Over the years it has been easy for unbelievers to blend in among believers, but there will come a time when your blending technique won't work. Don't wait to see if you have fully mastered your skills, but become all that God want you to be.

The purpose of becoming the temple of God is to allow Him to dwell within His people, enabling them to glorify Him in body and spirit. It is a habitation of God through His Spirit. The hidden secrets of God are revealed in the tabernacle. He will allow His people to flourish and prosper because this gives Him pleasure. Job states it plainly, *Oh that I were as in months past, as in the days when God preserved me; When his candle shined upon my head, and when by his light I walked through darkness; As I was in the days of my youth, when the secret of God was upon my tabernacle* (Job 29:2- 4). Ezekiel helps us also, he said, *Moreover I will make a covenant of peace with them; it shall be an everlasting covenant with them: and I will place them, and multiply them, and set my sanctuary in the midst of them evermore. My tabernacle also shall be with them: yea, I will be their God, and they shall be my people* (Ezek. 37: 26-27). Paul further told the people that this is a serious matter and not be taken lightly, because consequences always follow action. You are required to build upon the temple that has been laid for us. The foundation and the Chief Corner Stone is Jesus alone, and the other apostles and prophets have built upon that foundation. Somewhere along the line we have compromised our religious heritage and have fallen into a downward progression. We have lost the concept and forgotten to continue to build upon that which was already established by our forefathers, instead following our own desires. You are responsible for how you build and the materials with which you choose to build. When you release your earthen vessel into the hand of the potter, God will make you a vessel of honor and not dishonor. There remain some vessels of gold, silver, hay and the like. So yield yourself into the potter's hand because He only wants what is good for you. What will you use in your temple—gold, silver, or precious stones, which are eternal? Or will you add to your temple wood, hay, and dirt, which are temporary? Every man's works will be tried by fire, and made known—there is no hiding it. When we build with the right materials, we grow together into a holy temple of the Lord.

Don't you know that you yourselves are God's temple and that God's Spirit lives in you? If anyone destroys God's temple, God will destroy him; for God's temple is sacred, and you are that temple. (2 Cor. 3:6-17 NIV)

Failure to become the temple incurs the same punishment as destroying the temple, as both represent a failure to trust God with our lives. This is failure to complete the process that God had begun in you. If you don't complete the process you automatically destroys the temple because you are operating outside of the Holy Spirit residing in you. God has great plans for you. The goal should be is for you to become the temple and bring Him glory. Not to be made in the image and the image is never manifested is your life. He is the author and finisher of your faith but you have to give Him permission to finish the work. When we fail to execute God's plan, we are saying to God, "I don't want the success you have planned for me. I'm sorry, but you don't know what's best for me." On the other hand, when we destroy the temple, we are saying, "It is not that important if I ruin the temple. I only live once, and I am going to live this life to the fullest." Yet God says, I want you to prosper and be in health even as your soul prospers and that give Him pleasure. Jeremiah says, *For I know the thoughts that I think toward you, saith the Lord, thoughts of peace, and not of evil, to give you an expected end (Jer. 29: 11).*

Temple: The Body of Jesus

When Jesus went into the temple and cleared it of the merchants, along with the moneychangers, the Jews wanted to know: "By what authority do you clean the (physical) temple? And what sign will we have to prove that you are who you say you are?

Jesus said unto them, *Destroy this temple, and in three days I will raise it up* (John 2: 19). The Jews, obsessed as they were with the physical temple, wanted to know whether Jesus could raise the temple in three days, as it had taken their fathers forty-six years to build it. It was their sacred place of worship. John makes it clear that the temple Jesus spoke of was His *body* (John 2: 21). Jesus' physical body became a sanctuary for us to see, as it is in heaven. *For Christ is not entered into the holy places made with hands, which are the figures of the true; but into heaven itself, now to appear in the presence of God for us* (Heb. 9:24).

As we give our life to God we go from glory to glory, if your desire is to know Him in the fullness of His glory and the suffering of His death. We all start off in the same place in the outer courts. But then we must decide how much of a sanctuary we want to become. When we completely give our life to God we move from the outer courts to the holy place then into the holy of holies within the tabernacle. When we follow after and fulfill the desires of the flesh, we live in the outer courts. The flesh will kill you physically and spiritually if not subdued. Adam and Eve give us a perfect example of following the flesh and dying both physically and spiritually.

The instruction was given to Adam: *But of the tree of the knowledge of good and evil, thou shalt not eat of it: for in the day that thou eatest thereof thou shalt surely die*

(Genesis 2:17). In chapter three, the scene opens with the approach of the serpent, which offers Eve a piece of fruit from a tree. It started with a fruit, but the question then became: Who will be the smartest, man or God? Eve, forgetting it was God who gave her dominion and authority, gave room to the serpent and he planted a seed of deception in her heart. She allowed that spirit to take root and began to rationalize that she should be able to eat the fruit. Eve ate the fruit and gave some to her husband, and he ate as well.

It is clear that they regarded their will over the will of God. In the same chapter, in verse seven and eight, physical and spiritual death is manifested. Thus began the time when men's hearts and minds were open to evil and they hid from the presence of God. Hiding or wanting to leave the presence of God is a sign of spiritual death.

Anytime a person no longer wants to have an intimate fellowship with God, that person is physically and spiritually dead. The body is only alive if the spirit of God resides within you. Then if the spirit of God is not there you are spiritually dead. *For as the body without the spirit is dead, so faith without works is dead also* (Jas. 2:26). In Genesis 3:19, God announced their death: *For dust thou art, and unto dust shalt thou return*. In the book of Romans it says, *For if ye live after the flesh, ye shall die: but if ye through the Spirit do mortify the deeds of the body, ye shall live* (Rom. 8:13). Further, the Bible says *that no flesh should glory in his presence* (1 Cor. 1:29). Signs of spiritual death are fulfilling sensual pleasure, ignorance to the Spirit, and unbelief to the things of God, acting and living according to the standard of the world. This room is completely empty of furniture, and will require a proper spiritual preparation before entering the next room, the holy place.

For we know that if our earthly house of this tabernacle were dissolved, we have a building of God, an house not made with hands, eternal in the heavens. For in this we groan, earnestly desiring to be clothed upon with our house which is from heaven: If so be that being clothed we shall not be found naked. For we that are in this tabernacle do groan, being burdened: not for that we would be unclothed, but clothed upon, that mortality might be swallowed up of life. (2 Con 5:1–4)

This is the place where Adam and Eve found themselves naked and needed to be clothed. After they ate of the tree they were spiritual and physical naked. They understood that they were physically naked because they sewed fig leaves together to cover their bodies from God. To be naked in the present of God is no easy task. They did not understand that the fig leaves could not hide their spiritual nakedness. Before they ate of the tree they were clothed with the second meaning. Clothed, in this context, has two meanings: (1) having a body after the resurrection, and (2) being clothed with holiness, loyalty, integrity, honesty, faithfulness, and humility—just to name a few characteristic of a person robed with righteousness. Some of Adam and Eve new characteristics are disloyal, disobedient, dishonesty and pride were all exposed before God. The ones who continue to live in the outer courts will say, "It's okay if we go naked into the house of God—or even naked in the streets, as the ungodly do." We do not want to be found naked before God, but it is a process all men must go through. We are just like our forefathers, always hiding the truth about ourselves.

It takes great strength to say, "I am not Mr. or Ms. Goody-Two-Shoes." To be naked I have to admit that I have no power in and of myself and I'm not as great as I want people to believe. To be naked before God, we must understand how sinful our heart is, and how we are hypocrites. To be naked means no longer putting up a front before God but knowing that He sees me down to the joints and marrow. To be naked before God means understanding I'm not the one that's always right and everybody else is always wrong. It is impossible to come to this place of nakedness alone, because the Bible says every man is right in his own eyes. *Every way of a man is right in his own eyes: but the LORD pondereth the hearts* (Prov. 21:2). The author of Proverb also says, *There is a way which seemeth right unto man, but the end thereof are the ways of death (Prov. 14:12).*

If we go naked before God, then we have to admit that we are helpless sinners in need of a master. So become naked and admit that we are worthless without the power of God in our life and needs His skillful hand to move us to a new place in Him. Become naked and admit that our works cannot get us into heaven. Our works will bring us to the place of boasting about oneself. Your goal as a believer should be having a body after resurrection.

The Growth Process: No Skipping Grades, and No Shortcuts

Back in the fifties and early sixties, it was common practice that if you were smarter or more advanced academically than the other children in your age group, the school system would skip you a grade or two. But then school systems realized that by advancing these students, they might have hurt them more than helped them. They recognized that although the students were academically advanced, their fine motor skills were not as developed as those of the older children in their grade. The practice was then largely abandoned.

In God's plan, there is no skipping grades, no shortcuts and there are no promotions until the course is completed according to God 's standard even if you have failed a grade several times. The church like the Army preaches, no-man-left-behind, but the choice is yours to make whether to stay with the process or some one will be left behind.

The early church was the governing body of the community, and the world adopted the church's system of doing things. The twenty-first-century church thinks it can operate like the rest of the world, not leaving any man behind. They live like the devil and believe they still can get a promotion. Ministers preach that you are going to a new dimension, or that the next shift is coming now but if your life don't line up with the word don't look for this to happen to you. We adopt these words into our vocabulary and begin to think this applies to us even though our lifestyle has not changed. There is no advancing in levels or dimensions without achieving perfect growth on each level. If not perfect, you risk moving up before you have developed your fine motor skills. With the believers their fine motor skills are credible, respect, trustful, loyal, integrity and the like. When others don't see these characteristics in you, then you send to the world a faulty representation of Jesus.

Throughout the years, Christians have identified themselves in the Beatitudes and feel like they are doing fine and characterize themselves as such. For example, one may say about her/himself, "I'm a peacemaker," and so his favorite verse will be *Blessed are the peacemakers, for they shall be called the children of God.* (Matt. 5:9). The Sermon on the Mount was given to the followers of Christ to teach us how to live a Christian life. The promises and the word of God are given to believer so that they may have hope and encouragement through time of testing. In the natural tests are given to prove you have retained the information that was given to you. It also shows if you know how to apply that learned knowledge to your life. In the spirit tests are given for the same reason as the natural. Once the tests are passed it shows manifold purpose, which reflect Christ, help mankind-unspoken words, and develop the individual. A passing test proves your love and faith to God. It shows Christ to others and produces spiritual growth in you. Peter reminds us to, *Be glad about this, even though it may now be necessary for you to be sad for a while because of the many kinds of trails you suffer. Their purpose is to prove that your faith is genuine. Even gold, which can be destroyed, is tested by fire; and so your faith, which is much more precious than gold, must also be tested, so that it may endure. Then you will receive praise and glory and honor on the Day when Jesus Christ is revealed (1 Pet.1:6-7 TEV).*

This Sermon on the Mount is unlike the Sermon on the Plain, although some authors want to make them the same. Jesus was teaching his disciples the essentials of life, although there was many other people there listening as he taught. Without possessing these characteristics, one cannot become the disciple he was designed to be. The early disciples learned from Jesus' teaching and His lifestyle. To become a disciple today you have to continue in His word. The Sermon on the Mount gives you a step-by-step guide to maturity in the faith. Yet, as Christians, maturity is something we seem to be afraid of. Often we sell ourselves short instead of putting our hands to the plow and refusing to look back. We pick out one verse of the Beatitudes and claim that's who we are, instead of becoming the whole book. We accept the tricks of the enemy and compare ourselves with others. We wrestle with what we can't do, what we can't become, and what we did in the past instead of taking one day at a time and becoming a sanctuary that is pure and holy, a sanctuary where glory dwells. Each verse of the Beatitudes is a stage and the process, and you must go through each one if you are seeking a relationship with God. Although you may tote and quote the Bible, without a relationship there is no sanctuary or anointing to sustain you from the attacks of the enemy.

If you miss or misinterpret the key word of the Beatitude, then you will never get the full meaning of the whole sermon. We often get stuck on the word "happy," the promises, the meaning we want to take from the text, and forget the rest of the verse. When you fail to realize that you are helpless and in need of a Savior, you begin to travel the downward spiral. Instead of mourning for His presence, you drift farther away from God. Where there is no meekness there is no submissive, humble, or teachable spirit. Then the only hunger and thirst within you is to fulfill the lust of the flesh. The downward spiral leaves one believing only in oneself. It's all about me, myself, and I. This will only lead to the pride of life and the lust of the eye, which is Satan's stronghold. He tired these tactics with Adam and Eve and was successful. He also used these tricks against Jesus, but was not successful. We don't have to fall for his schemes. Jesus was tempted at all points but did not sin.

Understanding the Law of Progression

In the medical field a group of professionals join together to define problems and causes of problems within the organization. This program is referred to as *continuous quality improvement* (CQI). This team of professionals meets annually, semi-annually, quarterly, or monthly to discuss quality improvement. The purpose of CQI is to continuously monitor, evaluate, and improve the quality of healthcare given by the organization. So it is with the CQI team. They collect data in the problem area and develop a plan of action. In order to get the desired result, the workers have to implement the plans they have established. The team meets to discuss and evaluate the plan of care, whether it is successful or not.

Some of the business enterprise of this world has developed principles that follow the guideline within the Bible and they prosper in doing this. The Christian society forgot to develop these principles and they live in lack. In the life of a believer, we should always strive for quality improvement within our lives. The Holy Spirit reveals problem areas to each of us individually, just like the CQI team. The Bible contains the plan for improving our lives, but we have to study these interventions. We then have to move past studying the word to implementing it in order to get the desired results. From there, we are escorted into a new level and ready for our next assignment to improve our lives. Once we understand the process, life becomes easier, and we can look towards our goal, which is to walk in holiness. Each process involves learning how to give up a bit of yourselves in different area of your life. We have to get to the point where it is not all about us but about sharing salvation with all mankind. Your life is a mirror for all to see. If we neglect the correct process, then we paint a faulty representation of Christ. When the image of Christ is lost in our life, we will often create an illusion for the world, according to what they say we are. We are the one who are supposed to be changed. Walking in His glorious image and set the standard for the world. The process is a long one, and to the flesh it is an ardent one. But to the spirit, it is already won, because you are more than a conqueror.

There are always unbelievers around believers that make them believe the process of spiritual growth is over and often becomes a distraction to them. The process is not over until they are in the Witness Protection Program, their brother's keeper and bringing others along with them. The process is continuous and cannot be ignored or overlooked because of the inconvenient that it may cause the individual. The fifth chapter of Matthew, in the Beatitudes, Jesus gives the believers a promise through out each level of the process and the end is, great is your reward in heaven but you have to endure to the end. The Beatitudes give us progressive steps to monitor, evaluate, and improve our lives, making ourselves holy sanctuaries. When we talk about Beatitudes, we mean continuing to strive for the right position. In this context, "be" means continue, whereas "attitude" means position.[1] Matthew 5:3–9 are a call for Christians to develop a relationship with God, and it encourages us to know we are not of the world but are in the world. We are called to show the love of Christ to others. We are called to be a Christians and remember that we were once of the world, without a Savior. We should be merciful to non-believers and peacemakers to the world. Jesus is the peacemaker between God and man, and now we are to be the same for the whole world.

---

1 refer to note 2 at back

And, having made peace through the blood of his cross, by him to reconcile all things unto himself; by him, I say, whether they be things in earth, or things in heaven. And you, that were sometime alienated and enemies in your mind by wicked works, yet now hath he reconciled in the body of his flesh through death, to present you holy and unblameable and unreproveable in his sight. (Col 1:20–22)

We are commissioned to go into the entire world to preach the gospel and make disciples of men. But to make disciples, first we must be one. After becoming a disciple we can be to others merciful, prayerful, peaceful, and have the character of God. As an ambassador we have to show Christ.

In verses ten through twelve of Matthew 5, we advance through the process of becoming a mature Christian. When you are mature you can eat strong meat. This means that you receive the word as it is written and don't leave out parts of the word that you don't like. It also means that you must abstain from all appearance of evil. Once you have done this you can fulfill the responsibility that God has given you. You can forgive those who persecute you and speak all manner of evil against you. On this level, you can rejoice and count it all joy when you fall into various temptations knowing that the greater one live on the inside of you.

Dearly beloved, I beseech you as strangers and pilgrims, abstain from fleshly lusts, which war against the soul; Having your

> *conversation honest among the Gentiles: that, whereas they speak against you as evildoers, they may by your good works, which they shall behold, glorify God in the day of visitation. Submit yourselves to every ordinance of man for the Lord's sake: whether it be to the king, as supreme; Or unto governors, as unto them that are sent by him for the punishment of evildoers, and for the praise of them that do well. For so is the will of God, that with well doing ye may put to silence the ignorance of foolish men: As free, and not using your liberty for a cloke of maliciousness, but as the servants of God. (1 Pet. 2:11–16)*

The world will hate you and they will persecute you but, the most important thing to remember is that they do not hate you, but rather God, who resides within you. *The world cannot hate you; but me it hateth, because I testify of it, that the works thereof are evil* (John 7:7).

In these verses of scriptures there is a focus word in each verse. In which I will draw attention as the journey of becoming a mature Christian and reflecting the image of God.

Let's begin our process with the focus word in the third verse of this chapter: *poor.* The New World Translation Bible reads, *Happy are those conscious of their spiritual need or those who are beggars for the spirit.*[2] The word "beggars" does not mean that we should go to God and cry, "God, please God, oh please, please," but the word says, whosoever asks

---

2 Refer to note 1 in back

shall receive. The Greek word for "poor," in the Strong Concordance, is *ptōchŏs, pto-khos',* which means "beggar." Webster defines "poor in spirit" as the recognition that your knowledge is less than adequate. The first step in any recovery program is admitting that you need help. Whenever you are ready to repent of your sins and acknowledge that you are poor in spirit, that's when your downward spiral will reverse. Without knowledge of the word, you don't have the correct truth to believe and can't even imagine the truth. This process is coming to know the Great High Priest and to know that there is more to Him than you first imagined. The picture that you have in your mind of the true God is often distorted. That picture came into being when you tried to worship or live for God without being filled with the Holy Spirit. This representation continues when you tried to reason God out in your finite and without the leading of His Spirit. God is infinite and they that worship Him must worship Him in spirit and in truth. As you follow the process and mature, the real God will become manifest to you, and you will really appreciate His love for you and the new life He has given you.

Certain situations in life bring us to a lonely place where we feel life is no longer worth living. In the book of Acts, the jailer that was guarding Paul and Silas in the inner prison soon came to that place in his life. When he awakened and saw that the prison doors were open, he thought that the prisoners had escaped and wanted to take his own life. Paul told him not to bring any harm to himself. At this, the jailer cast off his state of hopeless and asked, "What must I do to be saved?" This is the beginning of the process—when you know that you are hopeless and that only God can help you.

> *And the keeper of the prison awaking out of his sleep, and seeing the prison doors open, he drew out his sword, and would have killed himself, supposing that the prisoners had been fled. But Paul cried with a loud voice, saying, Do thyself no harm: for we are all here. Then he called for a light, and sprang in, and came trembling, and fell down before Paul and Silas, And brought them out, and said, Sirs, what must I do to be saved? (Acts 16:27—30)*

Next, in the following verse our attention is drawn to the word "mourn." In the Strong, the word mourn is defined by the Greek as *pĕnthĕō, pen-theh'o*, which means "to grieve." Webster defines "mourn as to grieve for more." There is an epidemic around this nation that people of all age, ethnicity, and social background grieve for more worldly goods. They grieve for more money, power, and fame with one goal in mind and that is to have the most and the best of everything. For some people, how they get to the top is not their concern but that they get there.

In this place, you find yourself wanting more of what you got the first time you experienced Him. That is why men and women get married—they started grieving for companionship from another party. After the honeymoon is over, that's when the work begins to become one. When the couple said their vows that didn't make them one. They begin to work everyday to become one and so it is with Christ you have to allow the Holy Spirit to work in you to become one with Christ. *But he that is joined unto the Lord is one spirit (1Cor.6: 17)*. I'm not saying that Jesus will not hold and shield you after you start wanting more of Him, but I am saying that this is the time when you show who is the master and you must submit to His will.

This is the place where your spirit meets with Him in His Spirit and you begin to grieve for more. You knowing that-that one filling, that one-day of fellowship, or that one day in His presence was not enough. The fact of it is, that first one was filled with so much peace, pleasure, and calmness unlike any other thing in the world. His very presence put hope back into my living soul. From this experience I grieved for more of Him and started seeking after Him. That experience that you had the first time is not all there is to the indwelling of His presence. I can understand Matt.13: 44-46 is speaking of, *Again, the Kingdom of heaven is like unto treasure hid in a field; the which when a man hath found, he hideth, and for joy thereof goeth and selleth all that he hath, and buyeth that field. Again the Kingdom of heaven is like unto a merchant man, seeking goodly pearls: Who, when he had found one pearl of great price, went and sold all that he had, and bought it.*

When Jesus came into the home of Martha, her desire was to serve Him and provide the best dinner party a man could have. In her mind, this was a kind thing to do. Her sister, Mary, had a different idea and a different desire. She sat at His feet, because she grieved for more of the word that He taught. Martha became irritated with her sister, because she was doing all the work but Mary was going to enjoy the dinner as well. Jesus told Martha that Mary sought the one thing that no man could take. *But one thing is needful: and Mary hath chosen that good part, which shall not be taken away from her* (Luke 10:42). In the Psalms, David understood the one thing that he needed. *One thing have I desired of the LORD, that will I seek after; that I may dwell in the house of the LORD all the days of my life, to behold the beauty of the LORD, and to inquire in his temple* (Ps. 27:4). Paul understood the one thing that he needed as well: *Brethren, I count not myself to have apprehended: but this one thing I do, forgetting those things which are behind, and reaching forth unto those things which are before, I press toward the mark for the prize of the high calling of God in Christ Jesus* (Phil. 3:13—14). The wrong desire to grieve more moves some people to want the things of God and not God Himself, as it was with Simeon in Acts. Therefore, when your focus is on the one thing and that one thing is Jesus Christ, you can begin to humble yourself before the mighty hand of God. Then you can say, "Lead me by the skillfulness of your hand, dear Lord, into your will."

Continuing with the process, in verse five, the key word is "meek." If there is no meekness in your life that means you are unwilling to allow Jesus to be the Lord of your life. This is a necessary ingredient for the growth process. If you were going to bake a cake you would need some type of sweetener to accomplish the task. The sweetener is never seen in the cake, but all who taste it know that it is there. So humble yourselves before the mighty hand of God, and all who see you will know the sweetener is there.

The Greek word for "meek" (*praüs, prah-ooce'*) means, "humble." *Whoever therefore shall humble himself as this little child, the same is greatest in the Kingdom of heaven (Matt.18: 4).*

Webster defines meek as "submissive. *" So don't be proud. Put yourselves under God's mighty hand. Then he will honor you at the right time (2 Pet. 5:6).*

Whenever we see our lives as hopeless we grieve for the happier state that we were once in. That's when we become submissive in spirit and recognize, "I do need some help in my life, for my ways are leading me to destruction." You must be submissive and accept the leading and guiding of the Holy Spirit. A submissive believer not only yield to the leading of the Holy Spirit but also will give up of ownership of his body, soul, and mind to the Master for reproof, corrections, and rebuke. A submissive person submits to the authority that rule over them. *Obey them that have the rule over you, and submit yourselves: for they watch for your souls, as they that must give account, that they may do it with joy, and not grief: for that is unprofitable for you (Heb.13: 17*). When those believers know more than their leaders and refuses to submit this is what happens, *For they being ignorant of God's righteousness, and going about to establish their own righteousness, have not submitted themselves unto the righteous of God (Rom.10: 3*). One of the biggest wars around the world among believers is over doctrine and theology. A submissive believer is a teachable person and is dependent on the Holy Spirit for clarity.

Apollos was a teacher and "fervent in the spirit," he came to a place where he said to himself, I don't know it all, and he was willing to learn from others. Apollos gave us an example of a meek person. He was a Jew, and eloquent speaker and knowledgeable of the Old Testament. He taught the word of God boldly in the synagogue from what he had been taught. Pricilla and Aquila called him in private to teach him the way of God more fully. Apollos graciously accepted the teaching from them and was a great help furthering the gospel. From what he learned, he was able to teach other Jews that Jesus was the only way. Be willing to receive the teaching and training from others believers but always listen to the Spirit. The desire to know about God and have more of God and His word is real. To be in His presence is a priority. Staying on track and not losing focus, you will continue to become that sanctuary that you yearn to become.

And a certain Jew named Apollos, born at Alexandria, an eloquent man, and mighty in the scriptures, came to Ephesus. This man was instructed in the way of the Lord; and being fervent in the spirit, he spake and taught diligently the things of the Lord, knowing only the baptism of John. And he began to speak boldly in the synagogue: whom when Aquila and Pricilla had heard they took him unto them, and expounded unto him the way of God more perfectly. And when he was disposed to pass into Achaia, the brethren wrote, exhorting the disciples to receive him: who, when he was come, helped them much which had believed through grace: For he mightily convinced the Jews, and that publicly, showing by the scriptures that Jesus was Christ (Acts 18:24- 28).

As we continue the journey for spiritual growth, a key step is "hunger," found in verse number six. The effects of worldly hunger are mental preoccupation, moral degradation, physical deterioration, and sin. When Jesus speaks of hunger, he is referring to a feeling that will lead to a more productive, abundant life in Christ.

The Strong Concordance gives the meaning of "hunger" (*pĕinaō, pi-nah'o*) as "to crave." Webster defines hunger as "a strong desire," "a craving or urgent need." Yet it is critical that we hunger and thirst after God and His word, and not the gifts from God. Simon practiced sorcery in the city of Samaria, convincing the people that he was someone great. After the preaching of Phillip in that city, many stopped following Simon and believed in the gospel of Christ. He himself believed, was baptized, and followed after Phillip everywhere he went. When Peter and John came to the community, they laid their hands on the new believers and they received the Holy Ghost. After Simon saw what was happening, he began to hunger after the gift. He offered Peter and John money if they would give him the power to lay hands on people and have them receive the Holy Spirit. (see Acts 8:9-17;20-24)

> *And when Simon saw that through laying on of the apostles' hands the Holy Ghost was given, he offered them money, Saying, Give me also this power, that on whomever I lay hands, he may receive the Holy Ghost (Acts 8:18-19).*

The person of the Trinity is more important than any gift. God rewards those who diligently seek Him: *But without faith it is impossible to please him: for he that cometh to God must believe that he is, and that he is a rewarder of them that diligently seek him* (Heb. 11:6). Seek God first and above everything else, *but seek ye first the kingdom of God, and his righteousness; and all these things shall be added unto you* (Matt. 6:33). God is the only one who can and will satisfy our hunger. *For he satisfieth the longing soul, and filleth the hungry soul with goodness (Pss.107: 9).*

One example of one who desired to know more about God is found in the book of Acts an Ethiopian enunch. Once the desire is there you will not just stop at the local place of worship, but like this enunch who traveled to Jerusalem for worship. To attend worship service only was not enough to fulfill his desire and it is not enough for spiritual growth. The urgency was so strong that after worship he read the word from the book of Isaiah. Unlike many believers of today, who fail to read before or after worship service he wanted to understand the word so he invited Phillip to join his chariot to expound on the word to him more fully (Acts 8:26-40). The body of Christ has an urgent need and yet many failed to acknowledge the need and follow after it. The urgent need for the body of Christ is to come to His presence and receive the revelation of Him.

The other part to hunger is to thirst. It is almost impossible to hunger without ever being thirsty. In the natural a thirst is a desire to drink liquid and it comes before the hunger. Often time the thirst is mistaken for the hunger and if you maintain your thirst the hunger will go away. When that hunger and that thirst are not properly cared for then starvation and dehydration will over take you. So like wise in the spiritual it is almost impossible to have a hunger without a thirst. Your desire for the presence of God comes before the craving for Him. The psalmist compares himself to a deer that longs for water. Another psalmist said his soul thirst and his flesh long for God like a man in a dry and thirsty land. His passion for God is authentic that his soul longed and desired to be in the presence of God once again. When that hunger and thirst is not taken care of then separation from God will take place. The dictionary defines "thirst" as a desire, or longing. When your passion is to know Him more and desire to be in His presence, this cannot be confused with the need for earthly things. Just as you hunger, you also must thirst for Him, and the desire is so real. When that hunger and that thirst are continually filled then that person will ignite an unquenchable thirst for God alone. Jesus opens the door for us all, *If any thrist, let him come unto me, and drink. He that believeth on me, as the scripture hath said, out of his belly shall flow rivers of living water (Joh. 7:37-38).* The living water that He will give to you is the Holy Spirit, which is alive, and He will live in you. I found that the more I have of Him the more I want from

Him. It is an addiction for me I long to hear His voice, to be in His presence and to worship Him. I know this may sound as though it contradicts the word in John (4:14), which says you "shall never thirst." One of the thing Jesus was speaking of the thirst to fulfill one's sensual desires. This is something different from your previous experience that thirst can be confused with restlessness or the need for solitude and or material things. Neither the calmness of a lake, the most beautiful mountain vista, rolling hills, or all the material things in the world can fulfill that thirst. The only way we can quench this thirst is by praying, praising, worshipping God in spirit and truth and come into His presence. God invited you to come and partake of His great feast that will give you more pleasures and satisfaction beyond your wildest dream.

> *Ho, every one that thirsteth, come ye to the waters, and he that hath no money; come ye, buy, and eat; yea, come, buy wine and milk without money and without price. Wherefore do ye spend money for that which is not bread? and your labour for that which satisfieth not? hearken diligently unto me, and eat ye that which is good, and let your soul delight itself in fatness. (Isa. 55:1–2)*

Isaiah gives us a guarantee that God will fill our thirsty soul with the water. *For I will pour water upon him that is thirsty, and floods upon the dry ground; I will pour my spirit upon thy seed, and my blessing upon thine offspring (Isa.44: 3): This water is the symbol of the Holy Spirit.*

Any man who thirsts or hungers is invited to come and partake of the bread of life. *And he said unto me, It is done. I am Alpha and Omega, the beginning and the end. I will give unto him that is athrist of the fountain of the water of life freely (Rev 21: 6).* Trying to fulfill all one's desires is a waste of time --- and we have wasted a lot. Ultimately the satisfaction that comes from fulfilling our spiritual needs is a free gift. That presence leads to wanting more, and the more you get the more you have to have to sustain you. It is not rest for your body, however, it is the rest that awakens and refreshes your spirit to the will and ways of God. But that rest is to the awakening of your spirit.

The spirit within you is trying to take your mind, body and soul into the presence of God to that place you are longing for. For example, let us look at Cornelius, whose thirst caused him to give to the poor. A Roman centurion, he was well respected by the Jewish people in his area. Being in the middle of two great forces, he knew it was against the law for a Jew to associate or even visit a Gentile. Yet Cornelius excelled in the grace of giving and his faith in God, because his alms had come up before God as a memorial. When the angel first spoke to Cornelius, he believed what he saw and heard, and he sent men to Joppa looking for Peter.

The following day he expected Peter to come to his home, and he had called all his relatives and close friends into his home to wait on him. He told Peter they wanted to hear all the words that God had commanded. Cornelius realized that by being in the presence of God's servant, who delivering His word, he was in the presence of God. Hearing the gospel preached for the first time, he and his household were converted to Christ. They undeniable received the Holy Spirit with the evident of speaking in others tongues and worshipped God. They praised God and were baptized with water. His thirst was so real, and still this was not enough! They asked Peter to stay with them a few more days. God is no respecter of Person, when your desire or longing is toward Him and mankind He will give you the desires of your heart.

> *There was a certain man in Caesarea called Cornelius, a centurion of the band called the Italian band, A devout man, and one that feared God with all his house, which gave much alms to the people, and prayed to God alway. He saw in a vision evidently about the ninth hour of the day an angel of God coming in to him, and saying unto him, Cornelius. And when he looked on him, he was afraid, and said, What is it, Lord? And he said unto him, Thy prayers and thine alms are come up for a memorial before God. And now send men to Joppa, and call for one Simon, whose surname is Peter: he lodgeth with one Simon a tanner, whose house is by the sea side: he shall tell thee what thou oughtest to do. And when the angel which spake unto Cornelius was departed, he called two of his household servants, and a devout soldier of them that waited on him continually; And when he had declared all these things unto them, he sent them to Joppa. … Then Peter went down to the men which were sent unto him from Cornelius; and said, Behold, I am he whom ye seek: what is the cause wherefore ye are come? … And he commanded them to be baptized in the name of the Lord. Then prayed they him to tarry certain days. (Acts 10: 1–8, 21, and 48).*

Giving to the poor is a sign of your love and compassion toward God and mankind and will foster spiritual growth in you. *Therefore, as ye abound in every thing, in faith, and utterance, and knowledge, and in all diligence, and in your love to us, see that ye abound in this grace also* (2 Cor. 8:7). Spend some time studying tithes and offering. Where there is hunger and thirst there is the opportunity for compassion, which God will repay. *He that hath pity upon the poor lendeth unto the LORD; and that which he hath given will he pay him again* (Pro. 19:17). God's payments plan outweighs every plan or thought we have ever dreamed of. There is no investment plan better than God's. He's never bankrupt, never forecloses or sells out, and has enough to go around to everybody who wants some.

Verse seven introduces a new level of compassion for all men, not just the ones you love. In the Strong Dictionary, "merciful" (*ĕlĕēmōn, el-eh-ay-mone*) is defined as "compassionate," the same definition found in Webster. Peter and John were going to the temple at the hour of prayer and saw a lame man lying at the temple gate asking for alms, which he did every day. As they looked upon the lame man with compassion they called upon the power of God, which was within them, and the man was healed. When we develop compassion for others, then the people can hear with their spiritual ears. Compassion for others will cause you to defy the odds, because greater is He that is within you than he that is of the world. The people wanted to make gods out of them, but Peter and John proclaimed that they were men, just as they were. A compassionate spirit points men to Christ, as it did with Peter. Peter's second sermon was so successful that thousands were added to the church afterward.

> *Now Peter and John went up together into the temple at the hour of prayer, being the*

ninth hour. And a certain man lame from his mother's womb was carried, whom they laid daily at the gate of the temple which is called Beautiful, to ask alms of them that entered into the temple; Who seeing Peter and John about to go into the temple asked an alms. And Peter, fastening his eyes upon him with John, said, Look on us. And he gave heed unto them, expecting to receive something of them. Then Peter said, Silver and gold have I none; but such as I have give I thee: In the name of Jesus Christ of Nazareth rise up and walk. And he took him by the right hand, and lifted him up: and immediately his feet and ankle bones received strength. And he leaping up stood, and walked, and entered with them into the temple, walking, and leaping, and praising God. And all the people saw him walking and praising God: And they knew that it was he which sat for alms at the Beautiful gate of the temple: and they were filled with wonder and amazement at that which had happened unto him. And as the lame man which was healed held Peter and John, all the people ran together unto them in the porch that is called Solomon's, greatly wondering. And when Peter saw it, he answered unto the people, Ye men of Israel, why marvel ye at this? or why look ye so earnestly on us, as though by our own power or holiness we had made this man to walk? (Acts 3:1–12)

Howbeit many of them which heard the word believed; and the number of the men was about five thousand. (Acts 4:4)

In this race the crown is given only to those who endure to the end. This race is not for me only to win, but I am able to help my brothers win as well. The race is lost when we think, as the world does, that it is all about me. When I think I'm the best thing that God has ever created then I deceiving others and myself. The race may also be lost because of fear, unbelief, and sensual desires (i.e., when our whole focus is on the self). In the past, our government has vowed there will be "no child left behind" in our school system. The teachers have to take different approaches from time to time to accomplish that goal. So must we, as the body of Christ, continue the process in order to ensure that no man is left behind?

David asked the question in Pss. 24, what man could ascend into the highest heaven or who could enter into the holy place into the presence of God. He answers the question when he said he that has clean hands and a pure heart. Now we can agree the process wouldn't be complete without the word pure given to us in the eighth verse of the fifth chapter of Matthew. Throughout each level, the process requires us to kill more of the "flesh" that causes our problems. In the Strong Dictionary, the word "pure" (*kathar*ŏ*s, kath-ar-os'*) is defined as "clean" or "clear." Webster defines pure as "unmixed with any other matter, "spotless, containing nothing that does not properly belong;" "free from moral fault or guilt." As Christians approach this new level, they understand that their life is an open book. Mary Magdalene is a positive example of purity. She is the only female follower of Jesus who is mentioned by name in all four gospels. Jesus set her free of possession of seven devils. She, along with other women, provided money to the ministry of Jesus.

Mary didn't waver but remained faithful to Him throughout Him dying on the cross, burial, resurrection, and thereafter. She waited with Jesus as He died on the cross at the hands of the Roman executors. She watched Joseph of Arimathaea take Him down from the cross. Mary sat and watched Joseph as he wrapped the body of Jesus in clean linen and put Him in the sepulcher. She returned to the sepulcher early on the morning of the resurrection to anoint the body of Jesus with some sweet spices. She was the first that Jesus sent to carry a message to the disciples, and she always performed the tasks that were given to her. Although fear gripped her heart, she remained steadfast in her devotion to her Master. Mary followed Jesus from Galilee to Jerusalem and back to Galilee, spotless in her commitment to follow Him.

Likewise, in our own lives, we must stay within our designated zone to accomplish the will of God. For more information, see Matt. 27:56–61, 28:1; Mark 15:40–47, 16:1–9; Luke 8:2, 24:10; and John 19:25,20:1–8.

The process lasts a lifetime; so don't rush it lest you shipwreck the vessel (1 Tim. 1:19). There are many sizes and types of vessel. Throughout the Bible, vessels are used to delineate people. Some vessels are for gold, silver, wood, earth, gold, and dishonor, which speak of the qualities of that person. Desire to be a vessel of honor, sanctified, and meet for the Master's use prepared to do good work. There are several types of vessels --- passenger carriers, cargo ships, and tankers --- but the purpose of each one is the same: to carry someone to their destination.

On every ship or vessel there is a captain. The main job of the captain is to steer the vessel. We as the body of Christ are the captains of our vessel, with the free will to choose our course. The captain gets his signal from the control tower. Shipwrecks are avoided 90 percent of the time if the captain listens to the control tower. However, you can avoid wrecking your ship 100 percent of the time if you listen to your control tower (the Holy Spirit). In the Paul' case, from the book of Acts, he was connected to the control tower. The people would not have wrecked their ship if they had listened to him. Believe in God as boldly as Paul and stand on your belief, *sirs, be of good cheer; for I believe God, that it shall be even as it was told me* (Acts 27:25).

So hold to your faith with a good conscience and don't let it become dead from lack of use. For us, wrecking our ship means abandoning the sound teaching of God. So don't say things like, "I have time to get it right," "I'm just like everybody else," "They are in the church and don't praise or worship God," "They are not living a righteous or holy life," or "They are still lying, stealing, and cheating." God said, "Not one of you all can tell Him how many passengers you are carrying." Nor can you tell me how much cargo you have on your vessel. Don't give up, don't give in, and don't fall prey to the enemy. Stop, pray, and hold to the promises of God.

The process is not over, and verse nine brings us another word to remind us of this. The Strong definition for "peacemaker" (*ĕirēnŏpŏiŏs,I-ray-nop-oy-os'*) is "pacificatory, peaceable." Webster defines the same word as "intercession" and "one who makes peace by reconciling parties at variance." Paul encourage us to communicate with God for others which is vital for life. *I exhort therefore, that, first of all, supplications, prayers, intercessions, and giving of thanks, be made for all men (1Tim.2: 1).* Believers must value human life so much that they continually act as intercessors. Jesus asked me "What will we do at the beginning of the storm? Will we wait until the hurricane has spawned several tornadoes, or will we begin to pray when the storm is still in the ocean?" I understand you don't always know what to say just put your heart out there and the Spirit will intercede on your be half.

On the day of Pentecost, after they were filled with the Holy Ghost, many men began to speak in other tongues. Bystanders heard the noise and began to mock them and say that they were drunken men. Peter's spiritual inner man had grown into a place that he could reconcile parties at this point, and he was no longer that man that would curse others out or cut a man ear off. He no longer desired for blessing and cursing to come from his mouth, which is never pleasing to God. Instead he rose up and spoke to the crowd in order to show the people a new way. Many were saved on that day and were baptized with the Holy Ghost.

> *But Peter, standing up with the eleven, lifted up his voice, and said unto them, Ye men of Judaea, and all ye that dwell at Jerusalem, be this known unto you, and hearken to my words: For these are not drunken, as ye suppose, seeing it is but the third hour of the day. And with many other words did he testify and exhort, saying, Save yourselves from this untoward generation. Then they that gladly received his word were baptized: and the same day there were added unto them about three thousand souls. (Acts 2:14–15; 40–41)*

Peter was a man that desired to please God more than man and declared he cannot but speak what he had heard and seen. There was a time in Peter life that it pleases Herod to harass as many followers of Christ that he could. He put Peter in prison and his desire was to kill him like he had killed James because it pleases the Jews. While Peter was in prison being guarded by sixteen soldiers until after Easter, the church was interceding on his behalf. The night before the trail an angel of God came and escorted him out of prison into the city. Peter went to Mary's house where they were still praying and he spoken to them how the Lord had delivered and freed him from the hands of the enemies. The people around the world are still in need of some godly intercessor. Some parts of our nation are in the same state as Sodom and Gomorrah and unless men and women rise up with the spirit of Abraham and intercede for this nation then destruction in on the horizon. *Peter therefore was kept in prison: but prayer was made without ceasing of the church unto God for him* (verse five of Acts:12 see verses 1-19).

As a child growing up, once a year the movie *The Wizard of Oz*, based on the wonderful novel by L. Frank Baum, would be shown on television. Every year we would watch this movie. It was about this little girl who went to sleep and dreamed that she was caught up in a tornado. This tornado took her far away from home, and from that point her greatest desire was to return home to her parents. The little girl was told by the good witch to go see the Wizard, who would help her get home. To find the Wizard she had to follow the Yellow Brick Road. As she followed the Yellow Brick Road she came upon a scarecrow that needed a brain, and she welcomed him to go and see the Wizard with her. Throughout her journey to see the Wizard, she remained focused on her goal. She encouraged and welcomed a lion that needed some courage and a tin man who needed a heart. She interceded and did not withhold information that could have helped any of these companions reach their potential, but she encouraged them to do the same as she was doing. They each had a different need from the Wizard, and she took them along with her. In the end they unified themselves to help each other. They shared their faith with one another, uniting as one body, one mind with one goal.

The church has lost their concept and enthusiasm of developing a unified body of Christ. Unity will be complete when Christ is the center, which will change the course of this earth into the Kingdom of God in the earth. Unity is a sign of holiness, maturity, faith, and peace with God. Christ will return for that one body which is His church. Ever man thinks he needs his own church and it has to be the biggest church. This is a clear indication that he has the power to subdue and have dominion but he using it in the wrong place.

Many people tend to follow after or celebrate solo or independent performances. When most of the world's greatest accomplishments that can be seen are the results of teamwork where more can be done in less time. They live like the churches don't have to operate in diversity and unity. Remember the diversity and the unity of the Trinity. God the Father, God the Son and the Holy Spirit fulfill different positions and roles, but all work together to accomplish the same goal. So it should be with the body of Christ: each member may hold a different position, but all work together for the unifying of the body. It takes each one of us operating in our gift to have dominion and rule the earth having things on earth as it is in heaven. It takes each one of us operating in our gift for us to understand the power and the authority that the Trinity possessions. It takes each one of us operating in our gift in order to produce the mind of Christ. Each individual has various needs at different time in his life while on the way to Jesus. Someone may need to be shown love while others may need to be shown patience. Then there are some people may need to see faith in somebody else to give them hope. Until we become true intercessors and a unified body of Christ, we will not be justified when we stand before the Righteous Judge, our King.

Our Yellow Brick Road is the Bible, the word of God. Don't allow your needs to cloud your mind and lose sight of your responsibility to help your brothers press forward. The early church (described in the Book of Acts) and the characters in *The Wizard of Oz* are both examples for us today. In the *Wizard of Oz*, each character began at a different location, but all needed help. For most saints, it is difficult to perceive that we didn't all start at the same place. In the spiritual, we all start at the same place, recognizing we need Jesus to help us. At the beginning of our conversion, because we are blind, we fail to realize how much help we really need, and this does not become clear until we mature in Christ. Within the process; because of circumstances, backgrounds, and our knowledge of the word, we do not all begin in the same place. For example, a minister may have been able to rejoice when he was persecuted, because he was taught that's what ministers do. Yet he has not come to the place of hunger and thirst for God. Different people will take different routes to reach the same goal. So when their process seems a little different from yours, don't spend time questioning their motives, but encourage them to reach the goal of bringing honor and glory to God. Strive to be more like Job, who was a perfect and upright man, who was willing to help his friends even in the midst of them accusing him. *I will teach you by the hand of God: that which is with the Almighty will I not conceal (Job 27:11).* David wanted to instruct and teach man the way that they should go to prevent them from making some of the mistakes that he made. He encourages them not to be like a stubborn horse or mule that refuse to follow the available help. *I will instruct thee and teach thee in the way which thou shalt go: I will guide thee with mine eye. Be ye not as the horse, or mule, which have no understanding: whose mouth must be held in bit and bridle, lest they come near unto thee (Pss. 32:8-9).*

When we look at the lives of Jesus' disciples, we might automatically think that they were unqualified to be in leadership positions. They argued over who would be the greatest of his disciples. They fell asleep on him when they should have been praying. They all forsook him and fled. Fear was common among them. They couldn't hold to the promises of God, so they ran and hid when the Roman soldier took Jesus as a criminal. They wanted the rights of God exclusively for themselves, and wanted to call down fire when Jesus was rejected. They said, send the people home when they are hungry and shut them up when they cry out for help. Regardless of what the other person looks like, or where they are in the process just know that God is not finish with us yet. Paul teaches us that the end of our goal is to be conformed to the image of Jesus and not be conformed to the world. *For whom he did foreknow, he also did predestinate to be conformed to the image of his Son, that he might be the firstborn among many brethren (Rom. 8: 29).*

By now, you're so deep in the process you can't turn back and can't put Him to an open shame, so keep your strive. Track and field athletics' train repetitiously on keeping there strive and there timing. If they are going to make it across the finish line first or the leading scorer in that event then they have to keep there strive. Just one drop of the baton or one stumbling of the foot and they have lost the race. Likewise it is the same in the Christian's world if you are going to become the image of Christ then it is vital that you keep your strive. Although persecution may and will come, don't lose ground by opening your mouth but keep your focus and perfect your strive in the faith. Luke, the author of Acts encourages us with these words. *Conforming the souls of the disciples, and exhorting them to continue in the faith, and that we must through much tribulation enter into the Kingdom of God (Acts 14: 22).*

Enduring persecution in the power of stillness exhibit the greatest standard of faith that can be found among man. In verse ten, the focus word is "persecute." The Greek word for "persecute" (*diōkō, dee-o-ko*) means, "to pursue, follow after, given to, ensue, or press toward." Persecuted from Webster define as to cause to suffer because of belief. For examples of this, see, 1Pet 1:7; 1Pet. 2:19: 5:10; 4:14-16; Jam.1: 12; 2Thess.1:3-5

> *Only let your conversation be as it becometh the gospel of Christ: that whether I come and see you, or else be absent, I may hear of your affairs, that ye stand fast in one spirit, with one mind striving together for the faith of the gospel. (Phi. 1:27)*

Stephen was a man full of faith and the Holy Ghost who received persecution gladly. He was appointed to serve the needs of the widows while the disciples continued to study the word of God and prayer. Along with serving the widows' needs, Stephen performed many miracles and great wonders among the people. Opposition rose among the men of the synagogue that Stephen had spoken blasphemous words against the holy place and the law. Yet they could only find false witness against him. After hearing the word preached by Stephen, they were more furious in their hearts than ever. They convicted and stoned him to death.

Stephen provides us with a perfect example of how to receive persecution. (see Acts 6: 5-7:60) Stephen's death is often compared to the death of Jesus Christ. While he was being stoned, he looked up to heaven and cried out to God to receive his spirit. He went even further, asking God to forgive the executioners of their sin. We know that the way to deal with persecution is to ask God to forgive those who have persecuted us. Jesus did the exact same thing. He asked His father to forgive those who crucified Him. There is no way you can follow this example unless you have completed the process outlined above.

Persecution will come and it is only a test of your faith. When the tests are given it is to produce a fruit into your life such as virtue, knowledge, temperance, patience, godliness brotherly kindness and charity then you shall not be barren or unfruitful. Trails come to show what you are made out of or what is your stand in life for real. *If thou faint in the day of adversity, thy strength is small (Prov.24: 10).*

In the natural, test is given to prove you have retained the information that was given to you. It also shows if you know how to apply learned knowledge to your life. In the spiritual, test is given for the same reasons as in the natural. Once the test is passed it shows manifolds purpose, which reflect Christ, helps mankind unspoken words, and develops individual integrity. A passed test proves your love and faith to God. It shows others to Christ and produces spiritual growth and character in you. Triumphs precede each passed test. Job was a man that feared God and avoided evil and he understood the reward after the test. *But he knoweth the way that I take: when he hath tried me, I shall come forth as gold (Job* 23:10). After Job's test was over he did come through as gold because he had twice as much as he did before the suffering. There is a poem I loved from "Streams in The Desert" daily devotional reading that I know it will benefit all readers and help you understand suffering. God promise to never leave or forsake you so He knows exactly what is happening to you. He knows that you can endure the heat.

He sat by a fire of sevenfold heat,
As He looked at the precious ore,
And closer He bent with a searching gaze
As He heated it more and more.
He knew He had ore that could stand the test,
And He wanted the finest gold
To mold as a crown for the King to wear,
Set with gems with a price untold.
So He laid our gold in the burning fire,
Though we would have asked for delay,
And He watched the dross that we had not seen,
And it melted and passed away.
And the gold grew brighter and yet more bright,
But our eyes were so dim with tears,
We saw but the fire—not the Master's hand,
And questioned with anxious fears,
Yet our gold shone out with richer glow,
As it mirrored a form above,
That bent o'er the fire, though unseen by us,
With a look of unspeakable love.
Should we think that it pleases His loving heart
To cause us a moment's pain?
Not so? For He saw through the present cross
The joy of eternal gain.
So He waited there with a watchful eye,
With a love that is strong and sure,
And His gold did not suffer a bit more heat,
Than was needed to make it pure.
Arthur Tappan Pierson

Paul welcomed, and even took pleasure in, the hardships associated with spreading the gospel of Christ. You have to stay focus on the process and continue to grow in order to welcome persecution and accept those trials that will come to challenger your faith. *Therefore I take pleasure in infirmities, in reproaches, in necessities, in persecutions, in distresses for Christ's sake: for when I am weak, then am I strong* (2 Cor. 12:10).

Peter encourages the believers that when we suffer for doing right and give an answer to men in the Spirit of God we testify to others of the goodness of God. You also demonstrate the Spirit of Jesus who laid down His life for some wicked, filthy rags like you and I.

> *But and if ye suffer for righteousness' sake, happy are ye: and be not afraid of their terror, neither be troubled; But sanctify the Lord God in your hearts: and be ready always to give an answer to every man that asketh you a reason of the hope that is in you with meekness and fear: Having a good conscience; that, whereas they speak evil of you, as of evildoers, they may be ashamed that falsely accuse your good conversation in Christ. For it is better, if the will of God be so, that ye suffer for well doing, than for evil doing. For Christ also hath once suffered for sins, the just for the unjust, that he might bring us to God, being put to death in the flesh, but quickened by the Spirit. (1 Pet. 3:14–18)*

Suffering in the wrong kind of spirit is not beneficial to the person that is suffering or to the on lookers. Just imagine the suffering of Jesus. What if He was evil or nasty while being beaten or even dying on the cross? Then there would not have been you or I to enjoy the benefits of His death and resurrection.

Therefore you must still give glory to your Master in the days of suffering.

In the eleventh verse (the final one we will examine in this chapter), the key word is "revile," a part of the process that we cannot omit. The Greek word for reviles, from Strong (*ŏnĕidizō, on-I-did'-zo*), means to "rail, reproach, or upbraid." In Webster, revile means "subject to verbal abuse." The best example of a person who could remain silence in the midst of being reviled, persecuted, tortured and tormented is Jesus Christ. He took all the pain and never said a word to His defense. He also remains quiet with us during our times of testing, knowing that we have within us all we need to pass the test and remain faithful.

Their strength is to sit still (Isa.30: 7).

The death of Jesus on the cross was not only a crucifixion of the body but also a crucifying and reviling of the soul. As the Roman Solider crucified Him, they tossed dice for His clothes and made a sign over His head meant to mock Him but in fact making a true statement. The onlookers scorned Him and the chief priests criticized Him because He did not save Himself from death. (see Mark 15:25–32) Along with them there was a thief on the cross beside Him, who reproached Jesus because He would not save the both of them. Satan will always attack the flesh, and if he doesn't see Christ in us he will continue to beat up on us. Once he sees Christ operating in and through us he will leave for a season as he did with Jesus. Jesus was not governed by earthly emotion, will, and mind for comfort. He crucified all that this world has to offer—the pride of life, lust of the flesh, and the lust of the eyes. *For all that is in the world, the lust of the flesh, and the lust of the eyes, and the pride of life, is not of the Father, but is of the world (1 Joh.2: 16).*

He remained focused on the reason He came into the world that through Him the world might be saved. He is now seated on the right hand of God the Father Almighty. Reviling is the last and final stage of the process. When we complete the killing of the body and soul, then we enter into the rest of God. There is a place of rest in God that grants God the occasion to work for us and gives us the peace of God. That peace is not governing by feeling but is dependent upon your prayer life and your faith in God. It's the rest we enter when we withdraw from all worldly activity and operates in the spiritual realms, with authority and dominance. We can follow God's provision and answers for our lives, despite the cruel blows we may suffer in life. This is only for a moment but the joy that await us surpasses the pain, heartache and despair of a season if you endure until the end. The goal can be obtained so endure without complaining and keep your mind on the promise giver. *In your patience possess ye your souls* (Lk.21: 19). Verse twelve of that same chapter give us great encouragement to keep your strive. *Rejoice, and be exceeding glad: for great is your reward in heaven: for so persecuted they the prophets which were before you.*

Rest

Rest, in a spiritual context, means finding peace with God through Jesus Christ. It is virtually impossible to become a new man, made after the image of God, without entering into his rest. This rest is promised to all who put their trust in God and obey him. *My son, forget not my law; but let thine heart keep my commandments: For length of days, and long life, and peace, shall they add to thee (Prov. 3:1-2*). This book serves as a reminder to believers that have Fallen Short of the Glory that they can hope again and find rest for their soul. Once the believers balance their lives with the Word and enhance it in His presence they can love and live again. God desires that all his children enter into this place of rest, in complete surrender and loyalty to him alone. According to fourth chapter of Hebrews (verses 1–4), they could not enter into that rest because of fear and because they did not have faith in the word, which they had heard. Spiritually minded is life and peace, therefore those that believed in the word came into the rest of God. Fear and unbelief, which equals disobedience, will lead us to the wilderness and leave us there. Push past fear to the place that you will pursuit God alone, and your behavior will exemplify the image of Christ in your life. Unbelief will make one ashamed and without hope, whereas belief allows one to enter into that rest that God has promised. Belief gives hope, and hope makes us unashamed of the gospel. The Bible encourages us to cease our own work and enter into his rest. So whatever you have said, you trust God to be in your life, just let Him be that to you and let Him have His job. What you do is a revelation to others of what you believe.

> *Come unto me, all ye that labour and are heavy laden, and I will give you rest. Take my yoke upon you, and learn of me; for I am meek and lowly in heart: and ye shall find rest unto your souls. (Matt. 11:28–29)*

There is a peace for those who have learned to rest in God. This peace can bring quietness to your mind and restore your heart to rest. *And the peace of God, which passeth all understanding, shall keep your hearts and minds through Christ Jesus* (Phil. 4:7). Rest, according to Concise Webster, means "a state of ease, absence of motion, a pause of labor or exertion, that which remains after removal of a part" are some of the definition. This definition perfectly describes what man needs to do in order to enter God's covenant rest. Make some changes in your lives and enter into that rest.

> *A)* move into ease = *Trust in the Lord with all your heart; and lean not unto thine own understanding (Prov. 3:5)*
>
> *But seek ye first the Kingdom of God, and his righteous; and all these things shall be added unto you (Matt.6:33).*
>
> *B)* absence of motion = *Stop working your way to hell by fulfilling the desire of the flesh such as: witchcraft, drunkenness, strife, envy, hatred,uncleanness and for more see Gal. 5:19-23.*
>
> Stop appearing like you are a godly person yet your heart is far from God.
>
> *C)* a pause of labor or exertion = A deliberate change of plans and end all deceitfulness. *In all thy ways acknowledge him, and he will direct your paths (Prov. 3:6).*

Labour not for the meat which perisheth, but for that meat which endureth unto everlasting, which the Son of man shall give unto you: for him hath God the Father sealed (Jn. 6:27).

D) that which remain after removal of a part= After the flesh is removed then man will yield himself into the skillful hand of a Master builder. The part that remains is a man with a transformed mind. *A man living in holiness and righteousness after the image of God (Eph 4:24).*

When we place our trust in God, and in the process to remove all our unwanted natural characteristics, then the holy man, or the priest of God, will come forth. For more information on spiritual rest, see Heb. 4:9–11, Jer. 17:7, and Isa. 30:15.In the rest of God, you will find that sometimes He is quiet. During those times you may feel as if starvation has taken over you don't allow the rest or the test to over take you. There is always quietness before a storm, whether it a storm of joy or a storm of troubles. The day will come when this earthly tabernacle is over. On that day we will enter into eternal rest—rest from pain, labor, tears, and the like (Rev. 14:13, Rev. 21:4).

The Water

It is your own face that you see reflected in the water and it is your own self that you see in your heart.
—Proverbs 27:19 TEV

Living in a city surrounded by a lake, I often pass it and witness its wonders. With every trip, I always look into the water to see the reflection. On some days there is a clear picture of the trees on the bank. On those days I realize there is no movement upon the water. On other days there is no picture, and on days when the water is moving the picture is distorted. One day while driving, I listened as God talked to me about this situation. He said that's the way it is in the lives of the saints—as long as they rest in Him, a clear picture of Him is shown through them. But on the days when we are consumed with the affairs of life, then others cannot see the picture of Christ within us. The picture of Christ in our lives is also determined by how synchronized your walk, your talk, and your will to His. I will leave this question with you. What picture do you see in your life? What picture do others see in you?

The example of water and tree perfectly illustrates man and God. The water is a symbol of the Holy Spirit. It is the Holy Spirit that lives within us. God promise that He will fill you with the overflowing presence of His Spirit. Jesus reiterates what Isaiah had prophesied earlier. *He that believeth on me, as the scripture hath said, out of his belly shall flow rivers of living water (Joh.7: 37).* Often you will see a tree planted by the riverbank. The movement of the water and the distance of the tree from the water determines the reflection that you see. If the tree is far from the water you will not get the full view of the tree in the water. However, if the tree is near the water you can see the full reflection of the tree. The water will reflect what is before it, but the great honor is not to the water but to the tree. The tree is admired in the water, but the eyes are drawn upward to see the majestic beauty of the tree alone. It is the reflection of Christ in our life that will cause men to look up to see how impressive our God is.

To our amazement it is not the depth of the water that determines the picture. It is all due to the stillness of the water. The reflection is not once a week, or is it a certain day or certain time of the day. The reflection should be seen every day all day long.

God showed me this picture one day and it blew my mind. While walking on the beach one day I started watching the water descend back to the ocean. As the waves water descends back into the ocean, the small amount of water that remains on the seashore reflects the sun and the clouds above it. The depth of the Holy Ghost in your life is not the issue so allow the spirit to shine through. It is not determine by the number of filling. It can be one fillings or many filling of the Holy Spirit. Some reflections of the Holy Spirit should show through your life daily.

Our lives are just like water—it reflects who or what is within us. In our life when the waves are raging and we are rowing there is no reflection from the tree. You will only get a full view of the tree if the water is completely still; you're in the right position and distance to the tree, which is right relationship. The image that others see in you depends on the relationship you have with Christ. When your life is not at peace and there is no rest in your life then man will see no reflection. When others see Christ's reflection in you, it brings you glory. The effect is the glory of God, which he has given us. *And the glory which thou gavest me I have given them; that they may be one, even as we are one* (John 17:22).

That glory is not for your boast nor keeps for your self, but it is for you to glorify God and exalt Him. Man is the glory of God. That transformation of being changed from glory to glory really takes time and not excuses. Let it be known that man only change if he completely yields himself to the Master. Man was given a free will and with that free will man can decide if he wants that transformation or not. The people's eyes will be drawn upward to see the majestic beauty of God. The glory and honor is given to Abba Father alone.

Living in the Office of a Priest

We are of the royal priesthood, have present your bodies a holy and living sacrifice. God said this is the position He desires us to fill, which that is your reasonable service. Our position is slightly lower than that of the angels. *For thou hast made him a little lower than the angels, and hast crowned him with glory and honour* (Psalm 8:5). That glory and honor is for the master's use. This office does not require long white robes trimmed in gold, but rather a lifestyle that will bring a change in the lives of others. We are not alone as we enter into this process. God has equipped us with the Holy Spirit to help us and you don't have to work for it but you have to submit your whole life. The challenge is merely to do it. Toiling and complaining will not help us to accomplish the task. We must completely and restfully trust Him to do the work through us as we abide in the Messiah.

Our purpose is to be fruitful, multiply, and replenish the earth; subdue it and have dominion over the sea, earth, and the air (Gen 1:26). Also in Psalms it says, *Thou madest him to have dominion over the works of thy hands; thou hast put all things under his feet (Pss.8: 6).* Let's look at these words: *dominion* and *subdue*. Dominion means authority and subdue means to conquer. God made man in His image and you have the mind of Christ. God has given man the ability to take control of our environment on earth and all living creatures in his place. God delegated this authority to man, making us responsible. Man will have to give an account of what have happened to the earth, plants, and animals. How will you give an answer to these great questions?

It is our responsibility to bring glory and honor to God by recognizing that it is His power and authority by which we do these things. Physically and spiritually, we are able to help the deaf to hear, the blind to see, the sick are heal, and the enslaved to be free. We were made to worship God in our daily lives. Jesus, the Great High Priest, did not disregard priests who were beneath Him. After healing the ten lepers He told them to show themselves to the priest and offer the gifts that Moses commanded for a testimony. It may appear to you that you have the position, the power, and the authority to govern over people the way you want to. Make should that you are always right with God and man because judgment day is coming.

To be a priest we must be a disciple, servant, and soldier. Disciple training is the development of one own life by the guiding of the Holy Spirit. *And ye shall know the truth, and the truth shall make you free* (John 8:31). The servant is not the master. Every man has a master over his life; either we are a servant to do good or we are a servant to do evil. We are not in charge of ourselves—that is what the enemy wants you to believe. When you believe you control anything, you operate in the spirit of error. The soldier intercedes on behalf of others. For a believer, prayer is an absolute necessity and vital part of life. *I exhort therefore, that, first of all, supplications, prayers, intercessions, and giving of thanks, be made for all men (1 Tim.*2: 1). The soldier takes orders from his commanding officer and carries them out as they are assigned. *No man that warreth entangleth himself with the affairs of this life; that he may please him who hath chosen him to be a soldier (2 Tim.2: 4).* The Christian's soldier consists of, *Put them in mind to be subject to principalities and powers, to obey magistrates, to be ready to every good work, To speak evil of no man, to be no brawlers, but gentle, shewing all meekness unto all men. For we our selves also were sometimes foolish, disobedient, deceived, serving divers lusts and pleasures, living in malice and envy, hateful, and hating one another* (Titus 3:1-3). Priests are busy serving and dedicating their lives humbly, patiently, diligently, obediently, watchfully, and faithfully. Every priest is ordained for man but called by God to perform the tasks pertaining to God. He offers sacrifice for his own sins and for the sins of the people.

Priests offer gifts and sacrifices. *For every high priest taken from among men is ordained for men in things pertaining to God, that he may offer both gifts and sacrifices for sins* (Heb. 5:1). As a New Testament priest of God, we may both offer gifts and make intercession for sins. God always hear a repentance prayer and be assured He will accept you and him that cometh to me. *I will in no wise cast out* (John 6:37). For some of the other prayers you need a high priest or intercessor to speak on your behalf because not all children belong to Him. The Old Testament priest went into the holy of holies to present the sacrifice, and the Lord met them there. The order is still the same—we must go into the presence of the most High God when we pray, worship, and offer spiritual sacrifice unto God. In the Old Testament, we went in the flesh and in the New Testament we go in the spirit. Our spirit is escorted into His presence. Just imagine how you look and act sometime yet the Trinity brings you into the presence of God and you look like you belong there. The principle of God remains the same. He has already spoken and establishes everything. He is a just God.

Thank you Jesus! Hallelujah!

Just as the priest in the Old Testament made sacrifice, so you must do the same. We are to offer sacrifice and praise, worshipping him and confessing his name before men. *By him therefore let us offer the sacrifice of praise to God continually, that is, the fruit of our lips giving thanks to his name (Heb.13: 15).* Sometime the priest give up being right in order to win right later. These are the people that get criticized for doing right but when the unbelievers get into trouble they are the first to look for them. *In meekness instructing those that oppose themselves; if God peradventure will give them repentance to the acknowledging of the truth (2 Tim.2: 25).* One sacrifice we must make is never compromising the word of God. He shall teach the people the word of God. *"A priest should teach what he knows, and people should learn the teachings from him, because he is the messenger of the Lord All-Powerful".* (Mal. 2:17 NCV). That means living your daily life as a new man in Christ Jesus, because this is holy and acceptable to Him. The flesh has to die daily, and unless you present it to God as a living sacrifice daily it will rule you and kill you. Once you become the sacrifice on the altar and God is pleased with you, then you will see the glorious presence of the Lord. God was pleased with Moses after the completion of the sanctuary, and a visible presence of God filled the house. *Then a cloud covered the tent of the congregation, and the glory of the Lord filled the tabernacle. And Moses was not able to enter into the tent of the congregation, because the cloud abode thereon, and the glory of the Lord filled the tabernacle (Exod. 40:34–35).* When Solomon finished the work in the temple, God was so pleased with him that the priest could not stand to minister, because the glory of the Lord filled the house. *And it came to pass, when the priests were come out of the holy place, that the cloud filled the house of the Lord, So that the priests could not stand to minister because of the cloud: for the glory of the Lord had filled the house of the Lord (1 Ki. 8:10–11).*

Priests have compassion on the ignorant and on those who do not follow Christ. *Who can have compassion on the ignorant, and on them that are out of the way; for that he himself also is compassed with infirmity* (Heb. 5:2). Priests pity and are gentle with those without knowledge of the Living God, as well as those who have gone astray. He remembers his condition before he was saved and the mess that God saved him from and is thankful to God daily for his brand new life. The priest also knows that he is not perfect and is capable of falling; therefore, helping others is a joy. You have to communicate and practice fellowship with others in order to share the word of God and to change lives. He, therefore, will not judge anyone.

Priests are like Jesus Christ; they bring glory and honor not to themselves but to their Father.

Outer Courts

The outer courts represents those people who did not leave it all on the altar. They constantly repent with their mouth but remain in sin. They believe there is a god, or maybe they are god themselves, or there is a higher being somewhere, but nowhere to be found. Then they *enter into his gates with thanksgiving, and into his courts with praise: be thankful unto him, and bless his name* (Pss. 100:4). Those people render thanksgiving and praise to God just like they see the other believers doing. Often those people believes that because they are in the outer courts, there relationship with Jesus is okay or they have moved to the top of their relationship. They have forgotten that they who worship Him must worship Him in spirit and in truth. Have you forgotten that this is the area of the temple that God said not to measure, because it was given to the unbelievers? There are other levels to the relationship with Christ and other courts into the sanctuary. After you have accepted Christ, stand at the door of the holy place, ask God to reveal you to yourself so that you may hear Him speak to you. When we come to God in an unholy manner our sins are upon us, and sins cause disgrace and painful guilt and it hurts. The cost of sin is death, and nobody want their sins exposed before God; that's why it is hard to get naked before Him, as was the case with Adam and Eve.

Adam and Eve were our fore parents, who lived in the Garden of Eden. God told them to eat everything in the garden except that from the tree in the middle. Eve was deceived by the serpent (along with her husband) into thinking she would be just like God, knowing good and evil. Eve forgot she was like God, created in his image. This is why she fell into the serpent's trap; she ate of the tree of good and evil and gave some of it to her husband, and he ate it also.

After eating from the tree they realized they were naked and sewed fig leaves together to cover themselves from their pain, guilt, and shame. *Blessed is he that watcheth, and keepeth his garments, lest he walk naked, and they see his shame* (Rev. 16: 15a). In the cool of the day, when they should've been joyful to be in His presence instead they hide. God came to visit with them, they said to God, *because I was naked; and I hid myself* (Gen. 3:1-10). Before they sinned, nakedness was not a problem. Sin exposes your nakedness, your unworthiness to have a relationship with a worthy God.

We want to be clothed with our house, which comes from heaven, but there is a process and it costs you dearly (2 Cor. 5:1–4). Clothed, in this context, has two meaning: The first is having a body after the resurrection. The second is being clothed with holiness, loyalty, integrity, honesty, faithfulness, and humility—just to name a few characteristics of a person who is robed with righteousness. We don't want to be found naked before God. In the physical, some people believed it is okay to be naked as some come into the house of God, or even naked in the street, as the ungodly person. If you don't believe me, just take a look around your church on Sunday morning and see how sexually provocative most of your people are dressed. Whatever fashion the world dictates, that's what you see in the church house. Amazingly, you can tell a businessman from the worldly man in the street, but can't tell the worldly man from some of the believers any time. If you become naked spiritually, before God, then you have to admit that you are helpless sinners in need of a Master. To become naked you have to admit that you are worthless without the power of God in our life. To become naked you have to admit your works cannot get you into heaven; it is only by the grace of God that you may do so—and it is a free gift. To become naked you will admit that you are a filthy rag and then come to God with complete honesty, not trying to hide your past and present sins. To become naked before God, you have to look into my own heart and mind and see the real truth about myself. Those, issues that you have been hiding and running away from are revealed. To become naked you must know that God sees the real you, even down to every hidden part of you. *Neither is there any creature that is not manifest in his sight: but all things are naked and opened unto the eyes of him with whom we have to do (Heb. 4:13).*

In the outer courts, we learn that we have been anointed by God, have been called by name before birth, ordained for His work, and are of a royal priesthood. From the first chapter of Jeremiah it says, *Before I formed thee in the belly I knew thee; and before thou camest forth out of the womb I sanctified thee, and I ordained thee a prophet unto the nations (Jer. 1:5).* Paul told us that, *For we are his workmanship, created in Christ Jesus unto good works, which God hath before ordained that we should walk in them (Eph. 2:10).* All these statements are true, yet we find ourselves staying in the outer courts more often than we need to and do not desire to move beyond that place. The reason why we are called is for His glory; if we never move past this point we will never bring Him glory. The word says, *Even every one that is called by my name: for I have created him for my glory, I have formed him; yea, I have made him (Isa. 43:7).* We are called the righteousness to show others the way. *I the Lord have called thee in righteousness, and will hold thine hand, and will keep thee, and give thee for a covenant of the people, for a light of the Gentiles (Isa. 42:6).*

Our desire is that this will not be just another book to read, but that growth and the revelation of God may be revealed to our heart through this book, and using the Bible to go along with other books for clarification.

There are hidden mysteries in the Bible that are ready to be revealed to us, but we must be in the right position to receive the heart of God (Col. 1:26–27, Rom. 16–25).

Hidden Destruction

Sin carries within itself deadly venom. The venom is designed to make you destruct. Sin is deceiving and will make one operate on emotions rather than facts. Whenever we fail to fulfill God's plan and chase after the desire of the flesh, which we often feel is satisfying is often when we are headed for destruction. The DNA of sin is destruction.

Let us now look at the life of a man, named by God before birth, who stayed in the outer courts. His named was Ishmael, which means "God hears" or "God heard." He was the son of Abraham by a maidservant named Hagar. He received his name when his mother ran away from her mistress, Sarah, because of her rude behavior toward her. In the wilderness an angel visited her, telling her to return to the home of her mistress and give birth to her unborn son. The angel also told her to name the child Ishmael and that God would multiply his seed and he would be a wild man, for God had heard her cry. Hagar then returned to her mistress, Sarah, who later gave birth to a son (Gen. 16). As the child grew, Sarah asked her husband to put Hagar and the son out. Against Abraham's heart desire, he sent them away.

On the way to her home country, they ran out of water. Fearing that they would die of thirst, she placed her son under a brush and walked away, because she didn't want to see him die. Ishmael cried out to God, and He answers him. God sent an angel to minister to her again and provided water for them. He continued to live in the wilderness of Paran, where he grew up. His mother gave him a wife of her country, Egypt (Gen. 21:9–21).

As we see from the story of Ishmael, it is not enough merely to be called before birth. We have to search for the heart of God to walk in the will of God, according to His original purpose and plan for us. God wishes above all that none should perish, but the ultimate choice is up to us, because we all have free will. Yes, God heard Ishmael, and he stayed in the outer courts, which was as far as he desired to go. He lived as a wild man against every man, and every man was against him. Often we are like Ishmael; we don't seek the face of God. We fail to pray for persons, nations, schools, cities, and communities, leaving everything to God. We never lift anybody up before God but stand idle before Him. We just sit back and say, "God knows and He will take care of it."

Samson is another man who chose to stay in the outer courts. He was anointed before birth to be a Nazarite for life. Nazarites were separated, or consecrated, for the service of God and vowed not to drink from the vine, cut their hair, or touch the dead (Num. 6:1–6). Samson broke each one of the Nazarites' vows. He ate honey from the carcass of the dead lion he had earlier killed. He took a non-Jewish woman as a wife and drank wine at his wedding. Lastly, his wife unknownly by him had his hair cut off. Although God called you before your birth, you have to willingly commit your life to God. God has equipped us with everything we need to come into His presence.

Instead of setting the examples as a judge for the Israelites, Samson chose to fulfill the lust of the flesh and the lust for vengeance, and he was left in the outer courts. When he became a man he wanted a wife of the Philistines' people. This was in spite of his parents' guidance, and he knew he was acting against the will of God. Samson chose pagan wives (Judg. 14:1–4). So, during the wedding festivities, which usually lasted for one week, he decided to ask a riddle to some of his guests. He made a wager on the riddle—if any companions of his could solve it he would give to each man a sheet and a change of garment which total thirty men.

If they did not answer they would each give a sheet and a change of garment to him—and they all agreed. After the guests were unable to solve the riddle, they approached his wife for the answer. His wife got the secret of the riddle from him and gave the answer to their guests. In a fit of rage, he killed the thirty innocent men and took their garments to pay his wages. Because his wife had deceived him, he left her in Philistine and went home with his parents.

After his anger subsided he returned to Philistine to find his wife had been given to another man. He sought vengeance again, taking three hundreds foxes tying their tails together, then setting fire to them and burning their crops. The Philistine people burned his ex-wife and her father to death because of Samson's behavior. He then continued to war single-handedly with the Philistines, and later took Delilah, another Philistine, as his wife. Delilah agreed with the men of the city to find out the secret of Samson' strength, and she made these attempts daily. Samson made a game out of it; several times he lied to her, and with each answer she would call the men of the city to come and capture him. But to their surprise he would again show them his great strength. Yet she remained persistent, and one day she persuaded him to tell her the truth. When she discovered that his strength lay in his hair, she had his hair cut off. She then called the men of the city into the tent, as before, and to Samson's surprise his physical strength was gone. The enemy took him captive and put him in the dungeon. *And she said, The Philistines be upon thee, Samson. And he awoke out of his sleep, and said, I will go out as at other times before, and shake myself. And he wist not that the LORD was departed from him* (Jud. 16:20).

One day the Philistines had a festival in the temple to honor their god, Dagon, for delivering Samson, their enemy, into their hands. The people called blind Samson out of the dungeon to make sport of him in front of the thousands of people in the temple. Samson prayed that he might have revenge over the people of Philistine one more time, and then he would die with them. The little boy that guided Samson put him next to the pillar, as he had requested. He was then able to fulfill his heart's desire for vengeance by destroying Dagon's temple and the thousands of people inside.

Giving in to vengeance and the lust of the flesh always leads to destruction and ensures you will remain in the outer courts. The Lord will leave you in the outer courts, if that's your desire. Purposefully and willingly, give your life to Christ and you will continue to have an intimate relationship with him. When we no longer attempt to rule ourselves, but submit to the will of God, then we move into the holy place. We must be in agreement with the word: "Thy kingdom come. Thy will be done, on earth, as it is in heaven" and let it began in me.

Giving you this illustration of Samson, was done solely for an example of showing you what happen if you don't kill the flesh and reach your full potential. Samson is mention in the Hall of Faith and his faith was shown. The war he started David had to finish.

The Holy Place

The furniture in the holy place represents our life as we grow in Christ. First, the altar of incense represents dying in the flesh. The altar remains the place where killing is done. In the Old Testament, it was animals that were sacrificed for the sins of the people. In the New Testament, Christ died once and for all for the sins of mankind. Now, after the resurrection of Jesus, the altar is still the place where each servant must die to the desires of his own flesh, present himself as a living sacrifice and offer sacrifice of praise.

Secondly, the candlestick represents letting the life of Christ shine in us, or living a life of Christ. The candle of the Lord is like mirror, which allows you to look into your own heart, or conscience. The spirit of man is the candle of the Lord and He gives to man that inward light. Man is then equipped to think, plan, and weigh matters through the guidance of His Spirit. *The spirit of man is the candle of the Lord, searching all the inward parts of the belly (Prov.20: 27).* The Holy Spirit fills man and we become the light of the world. So that we may become as a shining light not only for ourselves but for the world around us. Light represents God's word (Pss. 19:8, 2 Pet. 1:19). *Thy word is a lamp unto my feet, and a light unto my path (Pss. 119: 105).*That light is made available so you can know yourself and repent through the guidance of the Holy Ghost. That same light is for the world, that you may show compassion, love, and kindness toward your brothers. *Then spake Jesus again unto them, saying, I am the light of the world: he that followeth me shall not walk in darkness, but shall have the light of life* (John 8:12).

In order to become the light we first have to come to the source of the light (Ps. 27:1, Prov. 6:23, Ps. 118:27). *I am the way, the truth and the light.* As you follow Him as the truth, He will bring you to life ever lasting. We are called to be the light of the world to show the people Christ. John came before Jesus to bear witness to the light, and now we are here to bear witness to it (John 1:7–8). Keep your lamp trimmed and burning so you won't be as the five foolish virgins. They gave out of oil for their lamps before the Bridegroom return.

Lastly the shewbread represents the bread of life. Shewbread was a part of worship in the Old Testament. Fresh bread was place inside the temple once a week. After taking the old bread out of the temple, the priest would eat it. Bread was offered along with an animal sacrifice. Shewbread symbolized God's presence among His people. It also serves as a reminder to the people of His ability to provide and sustain His people. To him that overcome doing it your way and yield yourselves to Jesus then you can eat of this manna, which is the bread of life. *Then Jesus said to them, Verily, verily, I say unto you, Moses gave you not that bread from heaven; but my Father giveth you the true bread from heaven. For the bread of God is he which cometh down from heaven, and giveth life unto the world. I am the bread of life. I am the living bread which came down from heaven: if any man eat of this bread, he shall live for ever: and the bread that I will give is my flesh, which I will give for the life of the world (Joh.*6: 32,33,48 & 51). Fresh manna was miraculously supplied in the wilderness every morning and enough to sustain them for that day.

In the New Testament we see the manna a little different and this manna is Christ. Jesus is referred to as the hidden manna, which is His presence with us but cannot be seen. Revelation says, *He that hath ear, let him hear what the Spirit saith unto the churches; To him that overcometh will I give to eat of the hidden manna, and will give him a white stone, and in the stone a new name written, which no man knoweth saving he that receiveth it (Rev.2: 17)*. You must worship Him in spirit and in truth. Jesus informed us that outside of this bread there is no life. We consume this bread when we partake of the body of Christ during The Lord Supper. This was the Last Supper Jesus ate with His disciples before His death on the cross. Not only do we eat the bread but also we eat of His flesh, *which is His word.*[3] This bread will forgive our sins and then give believers eternal life. Jesus taught His disciple to pray for this bread daily. *Give us this day our daily bread (Matt.*6: 11). In the natural, bread is needed for the physically body. In the spirit the bread of His presence is a must in our lives daily and the most important. Jesus reminders us in Matthew 4:4, *It is written, Man shall not live by bread alone, but by every word that proceedeth out of the mouth of God*. Daily bread is needed for our physical body and for our inward part of the spirit.

---

3 Insert footnote 4

Two Great Men

Here are examples of two men who moved into the holy place.

The first, Isaac, was named before birth, and the second, Samuel, was anointed Nazarite before birth. The name "Isaac" means laughter in Hebrew. When we come into an intimate relationship with Jesus, He will laugh with us. Isaac's life exemplifies living in the holy place. He was the promised son to Abraham in his old age.

The Bible states that God told Abraham to sacrifice his only son on a mountain that he would show to him. As a child, Isaac learned to be faithful from his father, as they demonstrated this great devotion to God. Abraham tied his son on the altar and raise up his knife to kill him. Just as he raised the knife, he heard the voice of God, which said, "Do the child no harm." At that moment, Abraham heard and saw a ram in the thicket. He untied his son and sacrificed the ram instead. Isaac continued that faithfulness into adulthood, when he refused to take an idol-worshipping woman for his wife. He trusted God and his father to provide him with a wife and trusted and prayed to God when his wife was unable to conceive a child.

Other characteristics of Isaac are submissiveness and a peaceful nature. We see this when there was enmity between his herdsman and Gerar's herdsmen over the well. Although they ran Isaac away from the well, he did not fight the herdsman back but dug a well in another land called Rehoboth. He had faith in God and believed they would be fruitful in that land. Upon moving to this new place, God confirmed that He would bless him and multiply his seed because of his father, Abraham. Isaac built an altar, worshiping and praying to God in that place. His peaceful nature was also evident when he made peace with the men who wronged him by causing him to move from place to place and dig new well (Gen. 26:20–25).

Other characteristics of Isaac include personal discipline, integrity, and humility. Meditating and patience were also strong attributes of Isaac and comparative to how Jesus waits for His bride, the church. Isaac waited for his bride to come to his homeland along with one of his servants. He trusted God to provide a wife and was in the field meditating when he saw her coming with the servant (Gen. 24:63). This is the attitude we will need if we are going to move into the covenant of Abraham.

Samuel ("name of God" in Hebrew) was another man anointed to be a Nazerite before birth. Samuel, while ministering unto the Lord (1 Sam. 3:1), heard the voice of God, calling him to service as a priest and a prophet (1 Sam. 3:7–10). As a priest he prayed and interceded for all the people of Israel (1 Sam. 7:5–6). Samuel preached repentance, entreating people to return to the Lord with all their hearts and put away their idol gods. Samuel told Saul, the first king of Israel, to go and smite the Amalek and destroy everything in the land. Saul did not follow the words of the Lord. He honored God rebuked Saul but not the position that he hold. He also rebuked the people about their choice of a king, because it was not God's choice. The people wanted a king, so God gave them one of their own choosing, and they chose one based on his outward appearance.

Samuel spoke the words of God as a judge in the lands of Bethel, Gilgal, and Mizpeh, and to all the people of Israel all the days of his life (1 Sam. 7:16). Samuel's two sons were just like the sons of Eli, and Samuel made them judges over Israel. Instead of serving God, like their father, they took bribes and were corrupt in their judgments (1 Sam. 8:2–3).

Holy of Holies

The only man in the Bible that was named and called a Nazarite before birth was John the Baptist. John's name in Hebrew means "God's grace." Before talking about John, we must realize that we are the same as John in that God has been gracious to us all. When Jesus was dying on the cross, the veil in the temple was rend from top to bottom. This signifies the yearly sacrifice of the high priest was no longer necessary. Believers can now enter behind the veil into the holy of holies at any time and in any place that they want to. *Which hope we have as an anchor of the soul, both sure and stedfast, and which entereth into that within the veil* (Heb. 6:19). At one time we were far away from Him. Christ's sacrifice of shedding His blood on the cross removed the wall that kept us from His presence (see Eph. 2:12–19). Now that the veil has been rent, we have access to the holy of holies.

Inside the holy of holies is the Ark of the Covenant, or the Mercy Seat. The Mercy Seat contained the Golden Pot with all its manna—Aaron's rod that budded and the tablets of the covenant (Heb. 9:4). The manna is the manifestation of God's provision for His people. That provision was enough to sustain them daily and have the presence of Christ with them. Aaron's rod budded signified that he was God's chosen one, and the tablets of the covenant signified God's word in our hearts. When we live a holy life, we boldly enter into the holy of holies (Heb. 10:19).

John the Baptist lived a desert life; he saw the spirit of God, heard the voice from heaven, and was uncompromising with the truth. He did not have the scripture as we do today, but he knew the voice and the spirit within him. That voice called him to rebuke, to correct and instruct in righteousness (2 Tim. 3:16). John spoke the truth to all men, regardless of class. Herod Antipas was the ruler in Israel and John condemned him publicly, claiming it was wrong to take his brother's wife.

For Herod himself had sent forth and laid hold upon John, and bound him in prison for Herodias' sake, his brother Philip's wife: for he had married her. For John had said unto Herod, It is not lawful for thee to have thy brother's wife (Mark 6: 17–18).

John said, follow the principles of Christ that will produce the characteristics of anew man, transformed mind and a clean heart. He said to the ones who had more than enough, give one of your coats to the one who has none. Not only did John preach holiness, but also he lived holiness, according to the testimony of Herod in the sixth chapter and twentieth verse of Mark. For Herod feared John, knowing that he was a just man, and a holy man, and observed him and heard him gladly.

Furthermore, Jesus told of John's righteous living, claiming no man was greater born of women (Matt. 11:11). John was a man of great humility and demonstrated it on several occasions. He taught his disciples, *I must decrease so that* He *can increase.* He was not in competition with the one that was to follow, Christ, and always pointed people to Him. *I indeed baptize you with water unto repentance* (Matt. 3:11–12). John knew who was the greater one so he encouraged some of his disciples to follow after Christ instead of continuing on with him. He remained steadfast in his expectation of Christ, even in prison, and his disciples continued to follow him while he was there (Matt. 11:2–3). He spoke out against people who lived unrighteous lives, who valued religious ritual more than true holiness. He acted as a light for men to see the coming Messiah. *He was a burning and a shining light: and ye were willing for a season to rejoice in his light* (John 5:35).

Your Calling Is Your Life

Who hath saved us, and called us with an holy calling, not according to our works, but according to his own purpose and grace, which was given in Christ Jesus before the world began (2 Tim.1:9)

Everything about you—everything you will do and should do—ultimately reflects your calling. Your behavior, work ethic, and personal goals should be a result of your calling in life, which will always put you in the Holy of Holies. When we begin to look at your calling and act on it, then you will have the mind of Jesus Christ. John the Baptist took his calling in life very seriously. From John's birth, he was determined to fulfill God's original plans for his life. I know that some people don't like God's original plans, but we as a body should want to fulfill it. His first plan was for us to have dominion, authority, and power over everything. Everything John the Baptist did was a result of the calling upon his life. John's father took his calling seriously when he prophesied over him at his birth. This is a prophet of God, he said, to prepare the way for Christ and tell the people to repent of their sins, for the kingdom of God is at hand.

> *And thou, child, shalt be called the prophet of the Highest: for thou shalt go before the face of the Lord to prepare his ways; To give knowledge of salvation unto his people by the remission of their sins (Luke 1:76–77).*

We should always rejoice when we think of Jesus coming back for the church or when we receive the mark of Christ upon our forehead. The question remains: What part of the church will you are found in? Will you be found in the outer courts, with the unbelievers, or will you practice being in the holy of holies before God?

> *I was then given a stick that looked like a measuring rod, and was told, Go and measure the temple of God and the altar, and count those who are worshiping in the temple. But do not measure the outer courts, because they have been given to the heathen. (Rev.11:1-2 TEV)*

Your love and relationship determines what area of the temple you will dwell in. *But the God of all grace, who hath called us unto his eternal glory by Christ Jesus, after that ye have suffered a while. Make you perfect, stablish, strengthen, settle you. To him be glory and dominion for ever and ever. Amen (1 Pet. 5:10–11).* The Almighty God has called you into fellowship with Him that He may bring you into perfection.

Witness Protection Program

Ye are my witnesses, saith the Lord, and my servant whom I have chosen: that ye may know and believe me, and understand that I am he: before me there was no God formed, neither shall there be after me (Isa.43: 10).

The witness protection program is designed to protect people before, during, and after that can bring definite testimony against criminals. Those in the program and their families are protected from physical harm and even death. Those who testify are given a new identity and placed in a new location, and they are forbidden from having contact with anyone from their past life. They may also receive a new social security number, money, a car, and a job. The program may be terminated if they break the law, give false testimony, or violate the contract.

We are looking for recruits to join our spiritual witness protection program. There is an urgency for believers to answer the call and join this program but don't look for many of your associates to understand the urgency. Although they see people dying and we think they are going to hell. Yet there is not an urgency to proclaim the gospel to the lost, hurting, and wounded through out all nations. This is unlike the government system, which does not value the testimony of children or people of unsound mind. God makes no such distinctions. If He did it for one, He will do it for all and if He accepts one, He will accept all. A witness always has the right to testify against him or herself, establishing it was the blood that freed them from the guilt and shame. You are commissioned to witness and show the praises of Him who hath called you out of darkness. This is a task that that can't be omitted but it is for all believers to proclaim the revelation of Jesus. We testify for the kingdom of God and against the prince of this world. Believers of Christ are to govern this kingdom and share with men of Christ great love for them. Yet the purpose of our testimony is to encourage and enlighten the hearer of our intimate knowledge of Him by way of things seen and experienced. Our protector has a hedge of protection around us, so that as the testifier goes forward no harm will come to him. The amazing thing about being in this program is you can testify about Christ's love and how he delivers you. Then you will continue to overcome all the sins that held you in bondage. The testifier won by the word of their testimony and the blood. Under the witness protection program for Christ, we are allowed to take on a new identity, because old thing have passed away. Our new identity points others to the one who allow us to abide under His shadow.

We make contacts with all our old friends and relatives because we would love to see no man left behind and they too can have a mansion awaiting them. The old man has passed away, and the new man has come forth with a penitent heart. We don't talk like we used to talk. We don't act like we used to act. And we don't dress like we used to dress. This book could not begin to cover all the benefits of His plan. Yet this witness protection program is still good. They world is waiting to see your holy living, your love, your prophetic gifts and your urgency working for them. Come and join today, the nations is waiting on you.

He that believeth on the Son of God hath the witness in himself (1Joh.5:10a).

References

New World Translation of The Holy Scriptures Watchtower Bible and Tract Society of New York, Inc. Brooklyn: International Bible Students Association,1988.

The Holy Bible, New International Version. Colorado Springs: International Bible Society, 1973.

The New Strong's Exhaustive Concordance of the Bible. Nashville: Thomas Nelson Publishers, 1990.

Webster's New World Dictionary, 2nd College Edition. City: William Collins and World publishing Co., Inc., 1978.

Good News Bible, Today's English Version. Nashville: Thomas Nelson Inc. Publishers, 1976.

Charles Caldwell Ryrie, Th.D., Ph.D. *Ryrie Study Bible, King James Version*. Chicago: The Moody Bible Institute, 1986.

Zondervan Dictionary of Bible Themes. Grand Rapids: The Zondervan Corporation, 1999.

New Concise Webster's Dictionary, New York: Noah Webster, LL.D. Editor-in- chief Edward N. Teall, A.M. and Modern Publishing 1988 Edition.

The Word, New International Reader's Version, Grand Rapids: Zondervan Publishing House,1995

Streams in The Desert, L B Cowman. Grand Rapids: Zondervan Publishing House, 1997.

www.ingramcontent.com/pod-product-compliance
Ingram Content Group UK Ltd.
Pitfield, Milton Keynes, MK11 3LW, UK
UKHW040556210726
13854UKWH00007B/249